MILITARY
Mom
on a
MISSION

MILITARY

Mom

on a

MISSION

An Advocate for Mental Health

Million Heir-Williams

XULON PRESS ELITE

Xulon Press
2301 Lucien Way #415
Maitland, FL 32751
407.339.4217
www.xulonpress.com

Unless otherwise indicated, Scripture quotations taken from the Holy Bible, New Living Translation, copyright © 1996, 2004, 2015 by Tyndale House Foundation. Used by permission of Tyndale House Publishers, Inc., Carol Stream, Illinois 60188. All rights reserved.

Paperback ISBN-13: 978-1-6312-9539-3
Ebook ISBN-13: 978-1-6312-9540-9

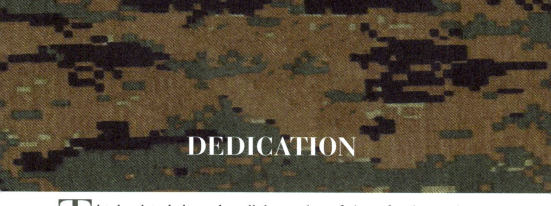

DEDICATION

This book is dedicated to all the mothers, fathers, family members, and friends who served in the military for this country. I have come to realize how family members are also negatively affected by military service. The following is a list of the American wars that all the unsung heroes fought in: Revolutionary War, War of 1812, The Civil War, Spanish American War, World War I, World War II, Korean War, Vietnam War, Gulf War, Iraq, and Afghanistan.

I dedicate this book to the first African Americans who served in the United States Marine Corps and became known as the Montford Point Marines. They confronted racism head-on and served this country with distinction and honor. USMC was the last military service to accept African Americans. I honor and salute you all.

My personal dedication goes out to my son, Jerome Bernard Milan Brown. He has endured the trauma of war and continues to fight against the mental affliction each day of his life. Jerome, you know you are my champion!

Next is my husband Stephen J. Williams, who served for twenty-seven years as a Marine and then worked seventeen years in civil service. We continue to stand together throughout this ordeal.

To my son Michael R. Brown, who is the rock of our family. My world would not be the same without my baby girl, Candis Grace Brown. She keeps everyone on their toes, especially me.

To my sister, Michele Reeves, who has always been with me through thick and thin.

I will always support my cousin/daughter P.J. who has been there for all my projects from the inception.

I give honor to my nephews who served in the USMC, LCpl Ramel McGowen-Dove and CPL Christopher Tate.

To my mother, Emma Grace McGowen, who always taught me the importance of never saying, "I can't."

Finally, I dedicate this book to my dad who served in the United States Air Force during the Korean conflict. My dad probably suffered from PTSD, unbeknownst to us all.

TABLE OF CONTENTS

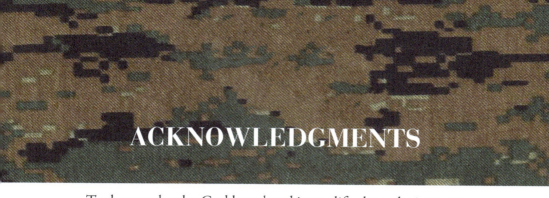

ACKNOWLEDGMENTS

To the people who God has placed in my life along the journey:

Montford Point Marines
Female Marines
Regimental Sergeant Major, Sergeant Major J.C. Haynes,
brother in Christ
Sergeant Major Harvey Lambka, USMC Ret., brother in Christ
Gunnery Sergeant LaShea Cavers, USMC Ret., bonus daughter
Tuskegee Airman, William "Joe" Johnson, a close family friend

Family members who have served in the Armed Forces:
Air Force Bernard McGowen, father
Air Force Henry Jr. Buchanan, uncle
USMC Master Sergeant Stephen J. Williams, Ret., husband
USMC PVT/E1 Jerome Brown, my son whose military life
is journaled in this book
USAF MSgt/E7 M. Reeves Ret., sister
USMC LCpl/E3 R. McGowen-Dove, nephew
USMC CPL/E4 C. Tate, nephew
Army SFC/E7 R. Seaman, cousin
Army SPC/E4 D. Green, cousin
Army B. Edney, cousin
Army Reserves SGT/E5 K. Vazquez, cousin
Army SPC/E4 M. Pittman, cousin
Army PV2/E2 T. Carter, cousin
Army SGT/E5 D. Gooden, cousin
Army PFC/E3 E. Alexander, cousin

Army PFC/E3 T. Alexander, cousin

Family and friends who have supported me
David James Albert Buchanan, uncle
Allen Buchanan, uncle
Shirelle Kunjufu, cousin
April Seaman, cousin
Deborah McCoy, sister in Christ
Priscilla Ratcliff, sister in Christ
Carla Ross, sister in Christ
June Hill, sister in Christ
Theresa Williams, sister in Christ
Marlene Jackson, sister in Christ
Troy & Diane Jones, sister, and brother in Christ
Shannon Jones, nephew
Debra Edwards, sister in Christ
Arthine Thomas, sister in Christ
Vanessa Ervin, sister in Christ
Lee & Grethel Humphrey, brother & sister in Christ
Pastor Vernon Roberts
Ed Brown, former Sheriff of Onslow County, NC
Catyana Brown, mentee
Billy Sewell, Owner of Golden Corral, NC
Barbara Ikner, former NC Onslow County Commissioner,
Chairwoman
Dr. Ron Lingle, former President of Coastal Carolina
Community College
Jacksonville, NC
Anne Shaw, Director of Economic Development & Business Center
Sistahood Connection, my Sista Gryls
Emergency Room Staff at Onslow Memorial Hospital,
Jacksonville, NC
MC Lyte, Hip Hop Sisters Foundation

Cheryl "Salt" James
Lyn Richardson, W.E.A.L.T.H. Vision 20/20
Fred & Kimberly Milner, prayer partners
Samuel Zhu, editor
Pastor Nathaniel Ford
Denaeya Brown, my playwright

The Scripture that kept me whole throughout this process reads,
"God of all comfort, who comforts us in all our tribulation,
that we may be able to comfort those in any trouble,
with the comfort with which we are comforted by God,"
(2 Cor. 1:4).

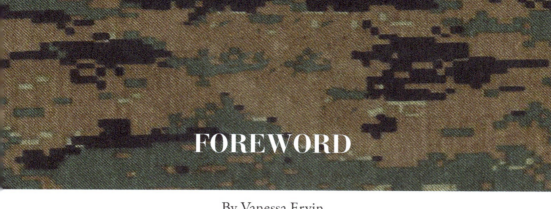

FOREWORD

By Vanessa Ervin

It was the "why" behind his unorthodox behavior that set his mother on an unstoppable mission to save her son. In *Military Mom on a Mission, an Advocate for Mental Health,* you will find a modern-day warrior in a mother who would defy the odds to expose the mental illness that had interrupted the destiny of her son, Jerome.

A warrior, or fighting spirit, is based on the confidence that positive steps can be taken in response to any stressful situation. That inferable strength is what Million-Heir Williams would discover in her quest to change the trajectory of an impending tragic outcome that is so often played out when families are confronted with the prevalence of mental illness.

For many families and military members, the associated stigma can be a deterrent to acknowledging the need for help. Those affected often fight their demons through alcohol and drug use. Post-Traumatic Stress Disorder (PTSD) and depression are two of three primary mental health concerns that may be encountered while serving in the military. The third is a traumatic brain injury (TBI).

As you experience the life lessons of this family, and those acquainted with PTSD, you will feel empowered to make a difference or encouraged that your tenacity to fight for your loved one is possible. I have often said to those who believe in the power of prayer and spiritual warfare that what happens in the natural is a false reading to what happens in the spirit.

Get ready to find hope and revelation that there is still much living to be enjoyed when you face the darkness. I know this personally as a mother with a son who is still facing his battle with PTSD.

Vanessa Ervin, MBA, MRA
Healthcare Administrator
Former Trustee of the American Hospital Association

Stay Connected to our Military!

IN LOVING MEMORY OF THE FOLLOWING PEOPLE

Emma Grace & Bernard Gisborn McGowen (parents)
Henry & Willie Mae Buchanan (maternal grandparents)
Patience & John McGowen (paternal grandparents)
Mae Anderson (aunt)
Bill Miles (bonus Dad)
Candis Brown (former mother-in-law)
Staff Sergeant Joe Williams US Army, Ret. (father-in-law)
Frank Ray (brother-in-law)
Anne Weaver (sister-in-law)
Linda L. Richardson (sister in Christ)
Former Congressman Walter B. Jones, 3rd Congressional
District, NC
Sudie Hobbs (Jerome's angel)
Former Councilman Jacksonville, NC Mr. Turner Blount & MSgt.
USMC Montford Point Marine (served 22 years in 3 wars)
First Sergeant Finney Greggs USMC Ret. (served 28 years)
Kynda Smith (sister in Christ)

THANK YOU TO THOSE WHO ENDORSED MY BOOK

Military Mom on a Mission is a self-help guide to assist anyone or their loved ones returning from war. It is engaging, informative, and very transparent. The timing of this book is impeccable considering the current state of our nation.

William "Joe" Johnson, Tuskegee Airmen Ret.,
United States Army Air Force

———◆———

Saying good-bye to a child leaving for the military is one thing, saying hello when they return is another thing. War changes you. How do you embrace a loved one returning from the military? Million Heir-Williams walks you through the pain, the horror and the hope of restoration. *Military Mom on a Mission* is a must-read for anyone who has had a loved one in the military.

Linda Olson, Bestselling Author of
Your Story Matters
wealththroughstories.com

———◆———

Military Mom on a Mission: An Advocate for Mental Health took me back to my entry into the military. It told the true picture of what a mother must go through when a child enters into military service, but it also shares what a child goes through to become a team of one. It also forced me to relive some challenging times when I returned from Southeast Asia. I was fortunate, just like Million Heir-Williams' son, to have a mother who was a rock and her son in Christ's hands. I think any mother or father who did not serve but has a child in the armed forces will gain insight into what's going on with their children, especially after they have been deployed to a zone they can't talk about. If they know how to pray, then please pray for them.

Grethel Humphrey PhD., SSgt. US Air Force Ret.,
Past Commander of DAV, Onslow County Chapter 16

The things seen, heard, and done on military tour is something that no one can imagine unless you have been there. Those thoughts are like a movie, continuously playing over and over in your head. Post-Traumatic Stress Disorder is a daily fight for normalcy for so many of our heroes as they return home. All you want to do is support, love, and help your child as they fight with internal battles in their mind, but you have no comprehension or direct understanding of what they have witnessed. What do you do? In *Military Mom on a Mission,* Million Heir-Williams expresses a mom's true love and devotion to fight the fight with her son, and for all heroes in need of help. For all families, friends, and loved ones of military heroes fighting with Post-Traumatic Stress Disorder, this is a must-read for encouragement, guidance, and hope.

Lyndsie Williams, LCSW

Introduction

WARNING...THIS BOOK IS NOT AIMED AT BEING POLITICALLY CORRECT!

My sister always said, "Have pen, will write," when a thought would come to me I would write it down. I wrote this book to help others who have dealt with, who are currently dealing with, or who are about to deal with the gruesome process of a family member returning from military deployment and war. The Holy Spirit inspired this book, so I can help teach others about the dark path and share what I have encountered along my journey as the mother of a veteran. The life as a military family was one of fear, loneliness, stress, desolation, gloom, and helplessness. It was a dimension that oftentimes was indescribable—and not in a good way. My son experienced Post-Traumatic Stress Disorder (PTSD) and my family walked that journey with him.

As moms, we live a mission when it comes to our children. My mission as a military mom, however, was quite different from my usual role as a parent. I went up against foreign forces. I did not have a script laid out for me. I did not know how to get my son the help he desperately needed post-war, but I knew I would die trying.

This book is for those who deal with mental illness and the families who experience the outcomes of its ugly aftermath. When mental illness is derived from war, DNA, or extreme trauma from everyday life's involvement, we are confronted with the same effects as if we went to war. Everyone seems to do the best they can with the knowledge they have as they navigate through mental illness. Since families are not trained to deal with mental illness, we can make matters worse because we do not know how to combat the illness in a positive way. I pray this book helps you as I pass along some advice that has worked for our family.

I am dedicated to taking the platform against mental illness and using my voice as an advocate for those who do not have a voice. It is long overdue for our culture to embrace and start removing the stigma that has plagued countless families in silence. Let us take up arms in the fight against this war on mental well-being. Mental illness has no boundaries.

Additionally, this book will also delve into racism and discriminatory practices of the armed forces that can contribute to the culture of mental illness.

To God be the glory as I sit in obedience to what I have been called to and purposed to do in life. Have a pen, will write. Have a voice, will speak.

Chapter One
IN THE BEGINNING

My children are the love of my life. Sometimes, however, they don't do what I think they should do, but I still support them. My eldest son Jerome Bernard Milan Brown joined the United States Marine Corps in 2002. It was a decision I disagreed with.

My story began May 1956, it was at this time that a creative force of matter was catapulted into the universe. This creative force was none other than me, Millicent Bernette McGowen. Born to the parents of Emma "Grace" and Bernard McGowen, a chocolate bundle of curly locks and smiles.

I was born two and a half years before my sister, Michele Rene McGowen. Not too long after Michele was born, my mom and dad separated. I spent my childhood in Glen Cove, New York—better known as Long Island. I was in the eighth grade when we moved to Locust Valley, New York.

My dad served in the United States Air Force and my mom worked for Helena Rubinstein, the L'Oréal of that time, for many years. Michele and I often spent weekends with our dad, so we always had a relationship with him. My dad always said, "Money is nothing but dirty paper." He had a money tree that sat on his dresser and he allowed us to take however much money we wanted. I remember Michele got a color television at the age of nine, and I received a typewriter for Christmas one year. Our Dad's motto was: Whatever my girls want, they get.

In his eyes, we deserved the world. Plus, money was nothing but dirty paper anyway. Michele cherished that color television. Many families didn't own a color television during the 1960s, nor were typewriters popular to have at home. My parents weren't rich, but we never went without anything we wanted.

After being medically discharged from the Air Force, Dad later became a baker. For his sincere love of baking, he was henceforth referred to as "Donut." Oftentimes, Michele and I would spend time with Dad at the bakery. The hot, melty, delicious donuts were the Krispy Crème of that time. The bakery was in Flushing, New York, which was located near a busy intersection and subway station. People were always in and out of the bakery. Michele and my friends enjoyed the luxury of receiving donuts we brought back for them.

Living on Long Island felt like a true suburban lifestyle in many ways. Growing up, Michele and I had talks about how our mother formed "a white picket fence" worldview. She lived as if everyone meant well, and she always demonstrated a giving and loving spirit to anyone who needed assistance. That worldview gave my sister and me a false sense of the real world. Our mom was quite overprotective in a lot of ways. She always made sure we had everything we needed. She enrolled us in a ballet class when no other blacks were exposed to that world.

Additionally, we lived in the neighborhood house. From my friends, to my sisters' friends, to my mom's friends, to our extended family, our house was always full.

I think this was because of my mom's loving but stern attitude, because if anything even remotely bad happened, my mom gave one of her "Mom Talks." Even when situations went right, she always provided wisdom to anyone in her presence. That was just the way she was. My mom always welcomed the world, no matter how life went. I never observed a time when someone needed help and my mom turned her back on them. We grew up with the philosophy that all things were possible and there was nothing we could not do.

The word "can't" was a curseword in our home. So, it was never used. Our mom always corrected anyone who said, "I can't." In return, she provided some wisdom. Nothing was impossible for my mom. She has always been the most incredible human being I have ever met. As an adult, I can reflect on so many great moments of her teachings and the character she displayed to the world. I have been able to duplicate many of my mother's gifts. My mother was a great entertainer, so there was always a lot of joy and laughter in our home.

One time, when I was a teenager, we just received a new car. It took place at the same time one of my friends, Derek, was visiting. He and my mother got into a conversation about how Derek needed to practice for his permit and how Derek's family would not allow him to drive. My mother opened the car door and told Derek to drive around the block to help with his driving skills. My mother kept insisting. After much persuading, Derek finally gave in and drove around the block. When he came back, he crashed into our driveway and dented the brand-new car. Even so, my mon still encouraged Derek. She told him it was fine and that everyone made mistakes. I am the way I am now due, in great part, to my mom's loving and extending attitude.

Growing up, Michele and I always got along. However, I do recall a moment in time when we had a physical encounter. After our mother finished with us, that was the last altercation we ever had. Michele and I have lived up to our mother's expectations. My sister and I have had disagreements, but we have never raised our voices or cursed at one another, and I do not believe we ever will. Our mom had a way of infusing love and respect into each of us.

I met my first husband, Rubin Rex, during my last year of high school. He was a musician in a band called Night Flight. The band played at a Glen Cove club named Christopher Street. Night Flight was one of the hottest bands in New York at the time. They were from Amityville.

Shortly after Rubin and I started dating, the band received a contract from Holland Dozier Holland (former Motown producers) and we headed to Hollywood, California. When Rubin asked me to move to California, I had some hesitation, but my last thought was, "What do I have to lose? If it doesn't work, I'll return to New York." If I did not go, however, I knew I would always have a little voice that would ask: What did you miss out on? I shed many tears at the table with my mother, but life was calling my name to the land of lights and cameras.

Rubin had a successful start in the music industry. He was a studio musician, so he played for several artists, including Jermaine Jackson, the Osmond's and had an opportunity to write lyrics for different artists. We lived a Hollywood lifestyle for a while and met a lot of people in the industry. I was on a few television shows, including *The Jeffersons* (Billy Dee Williams was on the set at the time), *Good Times* (when Janet Jackson was on the show), *One Day at a Time*, *What's Happening*, *All in*

the Family, and several others. My marriage was doing well, and Rubin and I had three beautiful children: Jerome, Michael, and Candis.

After the children were born, problems began to arise when Rubin's band broke up. He was a studio musician, so he got paid well and could work for anyone, but it seemed as though Rubin had a bout with depression. He started to drag me down with him.

Rubin eventually got a job with Air France, but he was still in a mental slump. One day, I thought, "I have a whole life ahead of me, and my children do as well. I don't deserve to be with a man who is melancholy no matter how I tried to fix it." I supported my family and felt like the weight of Rubin's depression wasn't my burden to carry. As a wife of many years, I still persevered. Nonetheless, the thought of divorce ate away at my soul. I was in silent anguish for years before I even began the divorce process. Our marriage lasted thirteen years, and our children are what I am most thankful and grateful for in life.

I always wanted a girl because I wanted to replicate the relationship I had with my mother. And I am very thankful for the strong bond I have with my children. We have a very transparent, trusting, respectful, and loving relationship. I am immensely proud of all three of my children for the character they have developed as people and the many accomplishments they have achieved. My daughter, Candis, owns her own marketing/branding firm. Michael owns his own real estate company. And Jerome is my war veteran.

I worked for Kaiser Permanente and Kaiser Hospital, in Los Angeles, for twenty-six years. During my tenure at Kaiser, I married Lucas, and we had a Hollywood style wedding in the hills of Griffith Park. Strange as it was, we dated for three years, but our actual marriage only lasted three months. I got out of that before things got worse than they already were.

I divorced Lucas because I *had* to. Looking back on my life, I realize I never asked God if He sent Lucas to me. I should have asked: "Did God put this man in my life to stay or was he just a lesson?" I now realize that Lucas was just a person who was put into my path in order to teach me a valuable lesson.

I furthered that lesson with my third husband, Freud. You never really know how far you can be mentally pushed until you completely break down. Freud did that to me. He and I got together in the summer of 1994 while I was in New York visiting my Aunt Mae. She was dying of cancer at the time. Aunt Mae was like a second mom to me. She never had any children and she lived with us for many years. So, I was in a very vulnerable state of mind when I met Freud. My cousin introduced him to me at a bar in New York. Freud was one of those fast-talking New Yorkers. He was very sophisticated, well dressed, and charismatic. Shortly after meeting him, I flew back to California. I was home for about a week when I remembered to check my voicemail. To my surprise, there were ten messages from Freud. I listened to all of them and although the first few were simple and formal, the remaining messages progressed into a jumbled haze of anger. Freud kept asking why I had not called him back.

At first I thought, "How dare you call and leave all of these messages on my phone. I don't owe you anything." I still called him back though. Freud apologized profusely and confessed that he missed me and wanted to see me. We were three thousand miles away miles away from each other, and I had no intention to start a long-distance relationship with a man I had just met.

After a while, we exchanged home phone numbers and started to talk more often. Eventually, Freud bought an airline ticket to New York for me. I really had a good time with him. Freud knew how to wine and dine a woman. He visited me several times in California as well. About six months after we started dating, Freud met my children.

I had no intention of moving back to New York. I was not going to move my children across the country. As time moved forward, Freud and I had a serious conversation about where our relationship was going. We decided that he would move to California. Freud and I got married, but things started to break down between us. He was a very argumentative person in which I was not accustomed to dealing with in relationships. This led to daily arguments which eventually led to disrespectful communication. I was faced with the decision to get divorced—again. My consciousness and my heart pointed me in two different directions, which is known in psychology as cognitive dissonance.

Freud would argue about the blue sky. It seemed like he couldn't be comfortable with our relationship if we weren't in an argument. My best comparison of him was the Pac Man. His constant barrage of words ate at me every day.

While I worked at Kaiser, I enrolled at Phoenix University and completed two years of classes in business management. As time passed, I realized the inevitable. Freud and my constant argumentativeness, combined with his love of drinking, pushed me to the breaking point. One day, I just could not take it anymore.

With three divorces under my belt, I still moved forward. I learned a great lesson when my mother died: Life still goes on. My mother had chronic asthma and throughout all her emergency room visits to the hospital, she always moved forward in life without ever losing an ounce of determination. She showed me that no matter what happens in life, it is up to us to show life who is boss.

Going back to my time at Kaiser, I worked as an appointment clerk in the eye clinic. One day, a coworker brought in a clip from a local newspaper. It read, "Models Needed" and had a phone number. The coworker said, "Millicent, why don't you call them. I think you would make a good model."

I laughed. "You have got to be kidding! This could be some kind of porn ring. I'm not calling those people!"

Nonetheless, she bugged me every day." Did you call them yet?" She would ask.

"No, I'm not calling them!" Would always be my reply.

After what seemed like weeks of constant badgering, I conceded and called the phone number on the ad just so my coworker would stop bugging me. When I finally called, I spoke to a woman who sounded legitimate. She informed me she was hosting a fashion show and asked if I would come in for an audition. I expressed to her I had extraordinarily little modeling skills and did not know if I was right for the job. She asked me if I was willing to learn some modeling techniques, and I agreed. What did I have to lose?

I went to the audition and to my surprise, it was very professional. I did very well in the fashion show even though I only had a few coaching sessions beforehand. Each fashion show I participated in after that, someone in the audience would ask me to walk in their show, too.

Eventually that little newspaper ad evolved into a part-time modeling career for me. It just goes to show that life is full of twists and turns and you never know where life is going to take you. I worked up to where I was in weekly fashion shows, and I traveled with a modeling troupe. We were based all over southern California at the time, and I had become a true celebrity on the modeling stage.

I felt at home on the stage. I got so much excitement out of watching the audience's response. The modeling troupe's commentator started saying, "Doesn't she look like a million on that stage?" After that, I was called, "Miss Million." Off stage, however, I was still Millicent.

I experienced a transformative change the more I heard my stage name introduced. I seriously considered legally changing my name. I didn't know the process to change my name, but I carried the thought of changing my name for about a year and a half.

On the evening of September 1, 1993, it came to fruition. I was immersed in a tub of hot water. I asked God, "Why am I still thinking about changing my name?"

The Spirit of the Lord said to me, "I have sanctioned your name change to Million Heir because you are connected to spiritual millions as a joint heir to my throne."

I sat there in total awe of the Lord's voice. He ministered to me about who I was. I laid back in the tub and digested His words. I let them permeate through my mind, body, and soul. I sat in silence for several hours and took in the experience I had encountered. It was life-changing to say the least.

Once I dried myself off, I wondered what it would take to legally change my name. I then wondered if people would accept or reject my name change. Then I thought, "I really don't care what people have to say." God had revealed the name change to me, so no man, woman, or child would be able to judge God's decision for my life.

The morning of December 16, 1994, I began the legal process to change my name. I went to the Superior Court of Los Angeles to file the paperwork. I received documentation of the name changes from the State of California, which was signed by the Secretary of State. The official filing took place January 13, 1995.

As time moved forward, the people in my life began to accept my new name. A few people refused to call me "Million." Each time I heard that, I responded "I will not answer to Millicent, so it is what it is." I told people I paid three hundred dollars to change my name and I was going to get my money's worth. Even though my name change upset some people, God always reminded me of several name changes that happened in Bible. Abram is the first biblical example. His name changed to Abraham. Jacob also became Israel.

I had settled into my new name and walked in the authority it gave to me. My new life consisted of Kaiser Permanente during the week, and fashion shows on the weekend. I was living my best life. The designer I worked for made the most exclusive pieces, and I felt like a queen on stage.

As time progressed, my modeling career began to wind down and I found myself on disability leave of absence from Kaiser. My doctor diagnosed me with depression. I was on call twenty-four hours a day for a full year. I was miserable. The mental stress that came with the job was astonishing. I oversaw two different departments, and I must have had forty-five people working for me. I was overwhelmed by their calls all day and night. That kind of mental pressure caused me to not only leave the job, but also to resign from Kaiser.

While on disability from Kaiser and divorced, I had no idea what would unfold in my life. I visited my sister in Virginia Beach. My cousin from Jacksonville, North Carolina, came to visit at the same time. I remember sitting at the kitchen table together for Thanksgiving. We ate shrimp egg foo young. None of us felt like cooking, so we decided to enjoy our time with one another. We talked about all kinds of things in life. At one point, my cousin turned to me and asked, "Why don't you move to Jacksonville? You're divorced, and you left your job already."

I looked at her as if she were crazy. "Why would you ever think a diva like me would move to North Carolina?"

Boy was I in for a shock of my life. Several months later, the Holy Spirit spoke to me. I heard the words, "It's coming from the east," spoken to me.

I eventually moved to Jacksonville to establish a business with my sister and cousin. We were going to open a transitional home. Since my sister and I had no experience in the field, our cousin signed us up for the Guardian Ad Litem program. The organization trains community volunteers to assist abused and neglected children in the court system. As a trained volunteer, we would become mouthpieces for those children as they made their way through the system. That is where God had me meet my God assigned, appointed, and anointed husband for life.

On the flight to North Carolina, I remember telling God on the plane that I didn't want to meet anyone, let alone date, and I certainly did not want a fourth marriage. Thank goodness God's plans are not our plans.

I married the most incredible man God could have given me. Stephen Joseph "Demetrius" Williams served twenty-seven years as a United States Marine. He retired as a Master Gunnery Sergeant. After serving his country for so many years, Stephen then worked civil service for an additional seventeen years before retiring a second time. That's true staying power. Kudos to my husband for all the times he stuck in there in spite of whatever was going on.

Stephen and I met at Guardian Ad Litem during a weeklong training. We were in the break room together, and I asked him, "Are there any clubs around here?" "I don't go to clubs," he replied. Our break ended and we went back to class. Three months after we met, we were married and going strong sixteen years later. Thank God!

While living in North Carolina, I opened my own business, which I started in my home. That business expanded to a storefront and eventually grew to the size of a warehouse. I enrolled in school again, this time with Liberty University. I attended online to get my bachelor's degree in psychology with an emphasis in life coaching. I also established a nonprofit organization that served women in the community. I became Vice President of the local Chamber of Commerce and became a County Commissioner. I was only the fourth female to serve in that capacity in Onslow county. I was also the first African-American female to serve and the first African-American, Republican, County Commissioner to serve in the entire state of North Carolina. Additionally, I was appointed by former Governor Pat McCrory to serve on the Board of Directors for the North Carolina Council of Women.

Aside from my three children, moving to North Carolina was one of the biggest blessings in my life.

LIFE LESSON ONE

My name is Million Heir-Williams. I did not always know where life was going to take me, but during my trials and tribulations I learned one thing: Keep it moving. It is not how you start the race, it is how you finish.

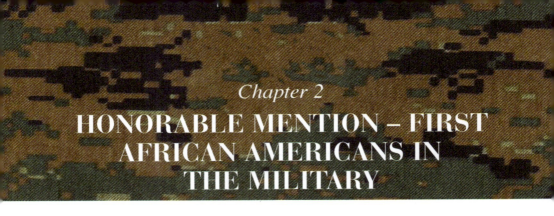

INCEPTION DATES

United States Coast Guard–August 4, 1790
United States Army–June 14, 1775
United States Navy–October 13, 1775
United States Marine Corps – November 10, 1775
United States Airforce–September 18, 1947

HONORABLE MENTION
Montford Point Marines

As an African American mother of a Marine, I thought it would be fitting to pay homage to the Montford Point Marines. They were the first African-Americans who were accepted into the USMC in 1942. Because of their sacrifices my husband and my son were afforded the privilege of joining the elite forces of the USMC.

As a former Onslow County Commissioner, I was invited to attend the Marine Corps Base Camp joint daytime ceremony celebrating the 240th birthday of the Corps at Camp Lejeune in North Carolina. As my husband and I took in the ceremony, I was excited because it was my first time experiencing a Marine Corps joint daytime ceremony. So many people were in attendance, and the whole crowd seemed elated. It was the most beautiful, sunny day in November on the east coast. For that time of year, it would typically be cold.

My husband and I watched as the history of the Marine Corps unfolded before us. Soldiers marched across the field as the commentator shared the Marine Corps' various wars and battles. One specific moment in Marine Corps history was highlighted: When women were first allowed to join the Marine Corps. It happened August 13, 1918, during World War I. Kudos to the progress of the Marine Corps for recognizing women and their ability to serve. When we got to 1942, there was no mention of the Montford Point Marines in the ceremony.

You might be wondering, "Who are the Montford Point Marines?" To my ignorance and naivety at the time, I certainly thought there would have been a proud African-American male represented in uniform to observe the first African-Americans accepted in the United States Marine Corps. Instead, I sat and watched as a white woman presented in uniform, and the commentator made honorable mention of women's acceptance in the Marine Corps. At that time, I would not have been allowed in the United States Marine Corps because my skin tone is melanin. So here lies a double grenade, the USMC accepting women, however, African-American women were not welcome to join as white women.

So, white women were accepted at that time, but African-American women were not. The righteous indignation of Christ began to rise up in my heart. My mind had to acknowledge what I just witnessed.

"Can you point out the General to me?" I asked my husband. "I would like to approach him about what I had just witnessed—or should I say, not witnessed—and possibly gain insight about what I just observed."

I could hardly wait until the program was over. As it ended, I was like an eagle in flight. I navigated myself onto the field toward the General. My husband and I met the General and stretched out my hand to shake his. I introduced myself as an Onslow County Commissioner, and my husband as a twenty-seven-year Marine Corps veteran. I also shared that our son served in the Marines. The General thanked my husband for his notable service. I shared with the General that the birthday celebration was my first time attending and that I enjoyed the ceremony—except for one part. He looked puzzled.

"Why were the Montford Point Marines never mentioned?" I asked. "It's as if its members didn't place their lives on the battlefield for this country just like their white counterparts." The General had a look of surprise on his face. I would imagine no one ever asked the General this question.

The ceremony we attended was held in 2016. The Montford Point Marines entered the Marine Corps on August 26, 1942. If my math serves me well, that means African-Americans served for seventy-four years and there was no mention of their service during the ceremony. This is all a part of the outcry of blatant racism in this country which we are tired of dealing with business as usual. This relates to why we are experiencing the fall out of George Floyd in Minneapolis, MN (I Can't Breathe). A Minneapolis, MN police officer by the name of Derek Chauvin held his knew on the neck of George Floyd, a forty-six-year old black man for approximately eight minutes and forty-six seconds which ultimately killed him on May 25, 2020. As a direct result of this occurrence, it sparked a global protest which significantly changed the trajectory of "Black Lives Matter!"

I cannot comprehend the blatant disregard for truth. The Holy Spirit often reminds me that God created my mind to be used for His glory and honor. God is the Spirit of Truth, so I must walk in the authority He gave me. I blame the Marine Corps for allowing a lie of omission to be perpetuated throughout history.

Why didn't the Montford Point Marines, the Montford Point Marine Association, and the community hold USMC accountable to reflect the "TRUE" history of the Corps? Having lived in Jacksonville, North Carolina, I had the opportunity to visit the Montford Point Marine Museum. Camp Johnson, NC is home to the Montford Point Marine Museum (where I lived five minutes from the base). How is it possible that a great memorial is on display to honor the Montford Point Marines, but the Marine Corps acknowledged nothing? I've had the honor of speaking at and being involved in several events held by the Montford Point Marine Association. If my dad, or another family member, served as a Montford Point Marine and wasn't acknowledged, I would have taken steps to rectify the situation. My dad served in the United States Air Force, and my sister also served twenty-one years in the Air Force. I already mentioned my husband and my son's service in the Marines. My family is intricately entwined with the Armed Forces.

I asked the Major General if it was possible to set up a meeting in his office on Monday? He directed me to speak with his Sgt. Major who was in charge of the ceremony. The Sgt. Major I spoke to was also the Sgt. Major for Marine Corps Installations East. Additionally, he was the Senior Advisor to the Commanding General for Marine Corps Installations East. I thanked the Sgt. Major and informed him I would wait for his follow-up call.

As a Commissioner, I did not take my job lightly. I took an oath in the office that included the well-being of the citizens at large. I deliberately spoke to each of the commissioners separately to gauge their true thoughts on the situation. They all agreed the ceremony's information needed to be rectified. I recommended we contact the Commandant of the United States Marine Corp to make honorable mention of the Montford Point Marines and to also have a physical representation of the Montford Point Marines in every ceremony to follow. The other commissioners agreed to send a letter to the General at Camp Lejeune that asked to amend the ceremony.

I anxiously waited for the next year's ceremony to see if African-Americans would be represented as the Montford Point Marines walked across the field carrying the Marine Corps flag with pride and dignity. An honorable mention of the Montford Point Marines was made by the commentator, however, an African-American was not represented in uniform to walk across the field. WOW, still follows up with the insult as to say, because you made an issue of the Montford Point Marine, we will give them an

honorable mention, however, we refuse to have an African-American walk across the stage to be represented in uniform.

It is apparent I am not a county commissioner currently. Therefore, I will schedule an appointment with the commandant of the United States Marine Corps and present this information directly to him to ensure it is rectified wholeheartedly throughout the nation. There is a Washington, DC trip in my near future.

I approached each of my fellow commissioners at the time and asked their opinion regarding the Marine Corps' ceremony. They all agreed the matter needed to be escalated to the Commanding General of Camp Lejeune. We wrote a formal letter and sent it to the Commanding General of Camp Lejeune.

Thank you to all my previous commissioners for joining me on this important piece of history, not only Marine Corps history, but also the United States of America history. Referring to this as only Black history minimizes the significance of human beings who honorably served and played an integral part of this country's overall history. I've never been okay with denying the truth, no matter who wants to disagree. Remember, silence is always consent in the dimension of evil and wrong doings. I will never succumb to that. No matter how uncomfortable it makes me or others around me, I was taught that right is right and wrong is wrong. There is a copy of the letter in the appendix section of the book.

I have personally known of a few Montford Point Marines. May God forever bless their courageous acts of heroism for facing war abroad and also right in the midst of the Marines and this country they vigilantly fought for. Thank you for standing your ground and not giving up, and for setting an example in the face of hostility and adversity.

It is worth mentioning that on November 23, 2011, President Obama signed a law to award all Montford Point Marines with the Congressional Gold Medal of Honor.

HONORABLE MENTION
Tuskegee Airmen

I am privileged to say that I personally know a Tuskegee Airman. He lives in Glen Cove, New York, where I grew up.

Below is an article in which Congressman Suozzi of New York interviewed Joe Johnson at his home and spent some time with him. The article tells the history of the Tuskegee Airmen.

Suozzi Presents U.S. Flag to William "Joe" Johnson, Tuskegee Airman and Glen Cove Hometown Hero

September 10, 2019

Discussed service to our country and overcoming racial barriers

On Monday, Congressman Tom Suozzi (D – Long Island, Queens) visited and spent some time with William "Joe" Johnson, a Tuskegee Airman and Glen Cove hometown hero. The Congressman presented Mr. Johnson with an American flag that flew over the U.S. Capitol. Additionally, he listened to the veteran's stories of his service to our country during World War II, the racial barriers that he had to overcome to become an aviator and his idyllic childhood growing up in Glen Cove.

"Joe Johnson is one of my hometown heroes. He personifies all that I love about Glen Cove," said Suozzi. "As part of the 'Greatest Generation', he persevered to overcome racial barriers and served our country proudly during World War II. 'Never Forget the Vet' is so much more than a hashtag. It is important that we sit down and listen to the stories of bravery and heroism of those who fought for the liberties that we enjoy today."

"Glen Cove was a wonderful community to grow up in. I lived on Cottage Row across from the church. There were ten in my family. We went fishing, swimming...I thought I was Huckleberry Finn," said Johnson. "I was the only black male in my graduating class. My teachers were great, even though there were no black teachers. I grew up with everyone together, especially the Italians."

The fourth of nine children, Joe was born in 1925 in North Carolina. When he was four years old, his family moved to Glen Cove to escape the racism that was so pervasive in the south. Johnson graduated from Glen Cove High School in 1943 and then joined the Army Air Corps. Growing up on Long Island, the "Cradle of Aviation", Johnson knew he wanted to become a pilot. He applied for the U.S. Army Air Corps flight training program and began pilot training at Tuskegee Airfield in Alabama in 1944.

After the war, Johnson attended college and then returned to his hometown of Glen Cove, where he raised three children. He worked at Grumman Aerospace for 28 years, eventually becoming a supervisor, and retired in 1990.

The Tuskegee Airmen were the first black military aviators in the U.S. Army Air Corps (AAC), a precursor of the U.S. Air Force. Activated as the 99th Pursuit Squadron in September of 1941 at Chanute Field, Illinois, the Squadron trained at the Tuskegee Army Airfield in Tuskegee, Alabama, becoming known as the Tuskegee Airmen. The squadron included pilots, navigators, bombardiers, maintenance and support staff, and instructors. During World War II, the Tuskegee Airmen flew more than 15,000 individual sorties in Europe and North Africa, earning more than 150 Distinguished Flying Crosses.

After the war in Europe ended in 1945, the Tuskegee Airmen returned to the U.S., where racial segregation remained the rule in both the U.S. armed forces, as well as throughout much of the country. Their exemplary service paved the way for the racial integration of the military. In 1948, President Harry Truman signed Executive Order 9981, mandating equality of opportunity and treatment to all in the U.S. armed forces, effectively setting the stage for racial integration throughout other areas of American society.

"When you were a Tuskegee Airman, the color of your skin didn't matter, the content of your character did," said Johnson. "I loved flying and the Tuskegee Airman gave me a chance, just like everybody else. It was my greatest adventure, and I am blessed to have been a participant.

HONORABLE MENTION
Buffalo Soldiers

"Buffalo soldier" is a nickname given to members of <u>African-American</u> <u>cavalry</u> regiments of the U.S. Army. They served in the <u>United States</u> from 1867 to 1896 and fought Indians on the frontier. The Indians gave the nickname. An 1866 law authorized the U.S. Army to form cavalry and <u>infantry</u> regiments of black men; the resulting units were the 9th and 10th cavalries and the 38th through 41st infantries (these four were later reduced to the 24th and 25th infantries, which often fought alongside the cavalry regiments). The law required their officers to be white.", (**Encyclopedia Britannica, 2019, Chapter 1**).

HONORABLE MENTION
Harlem Hellfighters

Harlem Hellfighters, byname of **369th Infantry Regiment**, originally **15th New York (Colored) Infantry Regiment**, nickname given to the 369th Infantry Regiment of the United States Army during World War I. The French government decorated the entire unit with the Croix de Guerre, its highest award for bravery, as well as 170 additional individual medals for valor. The 369th's battlefield prowess was almost overshadowed by its contribution to music, however, as the Hellfighters' regimental band was credited with bringing jazz to Europe", (Ray, 2019, Chapter 1).

A LOOK AT DISCRIMINATION FROM A PSYCHOLOGICAL PERSPECTIVE

As I continue to pursue my studies in the field of psychology, I gain new insights and understanding as it relates to human behavior during each class. I took one class called Multicultural Counseling, which covered discrimination, racism, bigotry. There is a specific field of counseling called Multicultural Counseling Therapy (MCT). The foundation of psychology is derived from a Euro-Western based philosophy, which negates the customs, values, culture, ideas, beliefs, and attitudes of minority ethnicities. As a result of these practice techniques in modern psychology, the field of Multicultural Counseling poses a threat to the institutionalized teachings that have been handed down generation after generation.

"As we have discussed, values of individualism and psychological mindedness, and the use of rational approaches to solve problems, have much to do with how competence is defined. Many of our colleagues continue to hold firmly to the belief that "good counseling is good counseling," dismissing in their definitions the centrality of culture. The problem with traditional definitions of counseling, therapy, and mental health practice is that they arose from monocultural and ethnocentric norms that excluded other cultural groups. Mental health professionals must realize that "good counseling" uses White EuroAmerican norms that exclude most of the world's population", (Sue, Sue, Neville, & Smith, Chapter 2).

"The definition of cultural competence makes it clear that the conventional one-to-one, in-the-office form of treatment aimed at remediation of existing problems may be at odds with the sociopolitical and cultural experiences of clients. Like the complementary definition of Multi Cultural Training (MCT), it addresses not only clients (individuals, families, and groups) but also client systems (institutions, policies, and practices that may be unhealthy or problematic for healthy development). Addressing client systems is especially important if problems reside outside rather than inside the client. For example, prejudice and discrimination such as racism, sexism, and homophobia may impede the healthy functioning of individuals and groups in our society", (Sue, Sue, Neville, & Smith, Chapter 8).

Many ethnic and racial groups experience higher rates of posttraumatic stress disorder (PTSD) as compared to White Americans. One explanation for this is the experience of racism, which can itself be traumatic. When traumatization is due to experiences of racism it is sometimes called racial trauma. Racial trauma can result from major experiences of racism such as workplace discrimination or hate crimes, or it can be the result of an accumulation of many small occurrences, such as everyday discrimination and microaggressions. An article by Williams and colleagues, published in *Practice Innovations*, aims to provide a context for understanding how racism can lead to a diagnosis of PTSD according to the 5th edition of the *Diagnostic and Statistical Manual of Mental Disorders* (DSM-5), (Williams, 2019, Chapter 1).

Theories of counseling and psychotherapy are influenced by assumptions that theorists make regarding the goals for therapy, the method used to invoke change, and the definition of mental health and illness. Counseling and psychotherapy have traditionally been conceptualized in Western individualistic terms that may lead to premature termination of counseling and underutilization of mental health services by marginalized groups in our society. The culture-bound values that may prove antagonistic to members of diverse groups include the following: focus on the individual, verbal/emotional/behavioral expressiveness, insight orientation, self-disclosure, scientific empiricism, separation of mental and physical functioning, and pattern of communication, (Sue et al., Chapter 7).

I have quoted aforementioned professionals in the field of psychology only to make a point of how it is known in the field that discrimination could almost be a tangible item to be viewed, observed, and placed under a microscope for investigation and research. It is apparent from my personal assessment that certain slang language can actually be formulated from a known fact such as, white privilege. It's clear to me, through my psychological studies, that white people oftentimes misunderstand the term.

QUOTES TO LIVE BY AND REFLECT UPON

I want to leave you with some thought-provoking quotes:

Dr. Martin Luther King, a Baptist minister and social activist, said, "Our lives begin to end the day we become silent about things that matter", (History.com Editors, 2009, para. 34).

Malcolm X, an American Muslim minister and human rights activist, said, "A race of people is like an individual man; until it uses its own talent, takes pride in its own history, expresses its own culture, affirms its own selfhood, it can never fulfill itself." ("Quotes by malcolm x," 2020, para. 10).

Harriett Tubman, an American abolitionist and political activist, said Harriett Tubman, said *I have heard their groans and sighs and seen their tears, and I would give every drop of blood in my veins to free them" (Harriett tubman historical society, 2020, para. 11)*.

Maya Angelou, an American poet and civil rights activist, said, "Hate, it has caused a lot of problems in the world, but has not solved one yet", (Goalcast, 2017, para. 19).

Oprah Winfrey, an American media executive, producer, and philanthropist, said, "Books were my pass to personal freedom. I learned to read at age three, and soon discovered there was a whole world to conquer that went beyond our farm in Mississippi." (Kniffel, 2011, para. 5).

Kerry Washington, an American actress, said, "You can be the lead in your own life.",

Kerry Washington, an American actress, said, "You can be the lead in your own life."(Hayes, 2015, para. 1).

Tyler Perry, an American actor, producer, and director, said, "It doesn't matter if a million people tell you what you can't do, or if ten million people tell you no. If you get one yes from God, that's all you need", (Meah, n.d., para. 1).

Damond John, an American businessman, author, and motivational speaker, said, "Don't focus on you, focus on what you can give others", (Leadhem, 2018, para. 1).

Sean "P. Diddy" Combs, an American rapper, producer, and entrepreneur, said, "Don't be afraid to close your eyes and dream but then open your eyes and see", (Robertson, 2014, para. 4).

Lashea Cavers, an American entrepreneur, retired Marine of twenty years, and legend of Onslow County, said, "Don't reinvent the wheel, improve the wheel", (Lashea Cavers, personal communication, February 2, 2020).

Jane Elliott, an American, former third-grade teacher known for her experiment, Blue Eyes-Brown Exercise, said, "We learn to be racist, therefore, we can learn not to be racist. Racism is not genetics. It has everything to do with power", (Jane Elliott, personal communication, February 24, 2020).

Carol Burnett, an actor, and producer, said, "Only I can change my life. No one can do it for me", ("Carol burnett quote," 2020, para. 1).

Nathan Rutstein, an author, lecturer, and college educator said, "Prejudice is an emotional commitment to ignorance" (Rutstein, para. 22).

Napoleon Bonaparte, a French military leader and emperor, said, "History is a collection of lies agreed upon by the victors." (Public Broadcasting Service, n.d., para. 15).

Dalai Lama XIV, a current monk of Tibet and Buddhism, said, "Peace does not mean an absence of conflicts: differences will always be there. Peace means solving these differences through peaceful means: dialogue, education, knowledge and through humane ways.", (Abhishek, 2017, para. 1).

Mother Teresa, known as Saint Teresa of Calcutta as acknowledged in the Catholic church, said, "If we have no peace it is because we have forgotten that we belong to each other", ("Mother Teresa Quotes," 2020, para. 17).

A. P. J. Abdul Kalam, the former president of India and an aerospace scientist, said, "Never stop fighting until you arrive at your destined place—that is, the unique you. Have an aim in life, continuously acquire knowledge, work hard, and have the perseverance to realize the great life", ("Dr apj abdul kalam quotes," 2016, para. 4).

Million Heir-Williams, an American author, entrepreneur, life coach, and speaker. My quote is, "Truth is a rare commodity, that only truth-seekers will unfold. My glass is never half empty, nor it is half-full, it is always overflowing."

LIFE LESSON TWO

Just because you have been invited somewhere;
does not mean you are welcome.
by Million Heir-Williams

Chapter 3
VACATION DETOUR

I n August 2002, I sat in the terminal at LAX airport with my three children. We waited for our flight to Virginia Beach. We were all excited because we would also be attending our family reunion in Jacksonville, North Carolina. We were to meet up with my sister, Michele, and her two sons, Ramel and Christopher, in Virginia Beach and then drive together to Jacksonville.

Once we arrived in Virginia Beach, we loaded up two vehicles and hit the road. All the country roads were beautiful. My children and I were not accustomed to all the open terrain due to living in Los Angeles. So, the change in scenery was euphoric for us. The deep emerald-colored trees, the bright sunflowers, and the fresh air—we could not get enough. I enjoyed God's gorgeous creations to their fullest, and it was such an exhilarating experience.

After a few hours, we arrived in Jacksonville. The city is known as the "Home of the Most Extensive Amphibious Base in the World." It was also home to the United States Marine Corps' Camp Lejeune base.

While in town, we toured the base, and I assure you it was a city within a city. Everything a soldier needed was on base: restaurants, grocery stores, gyms, swimming pools, and even a little beach. No one ever needed to leave base.

The trip to the south was the first for my children and myself. We spent several days in Jacksonville getting acquainted with the family and enjoying all the outlined activities of our family reunion. I had not seen many family members in years, and my children had not met several prior to the trip.

When the trip was over, we were sad to see the good times come to an end. Before leaving, we all exchanged phone numbers and addresses to stay in contact. We all wanted another trip as soon as possible. Before we knew it we were back in Virginia Beach preparing for our flight back to Los Angeles.

Little did I know at the time, my nephews spent a lot of time talking to my son about joining the United States Marine Corps. They had enlisted a month before the family reunion, and their excitement rubbed off on Jerome. He decided to join as well. My sister had considerable opposition to the Marines Corps because they were the first to go into battle. She did not want that for her sons or mine.

I had never enlisted, nor did I ever have a remote desire to join the Armed Forces. I was quite happy serving twenty-two years in healthcare management along with my various endeavors as an entrepreneur.

My nephews were in constant conversation with their recruiter and even set up an appointment for Jerome, who was twenty-three, to speak with the recruiter, too. Jerome signed the paperwork for the Marines. My sister did state that it was a good idea that Jerome at least joined with his cousins because they could take advantage of the buddy system. Plus, perks like free, higher education and excellent medical benefits were good for the three of them. We also were not in active war at the time. Had that been the case, I would have never agreed or supported my son joining the military, despite his level of enthusiasm. Additionally, since Jerome was an adult, I didn't have a leg to stand on.

When I think of a Marine, I think of the Terminator. Jerome did not have that type of demeanor. Before our family reunion, Jerome worked for a telecommunications firm in Downtown Los Angeles. He had enjoyed his career. Jerome had been a top sales associate a few times and wanted long-term plans with the company. He was mild-mannered, but very funny. Jerome enjoyed laughing as much as he loved living. If you are around Jerome, you are guaranteed to laugh.

As a child, Jerome never got in a fight, and he was never suspended from school. He was a very loving child. When we would say our prayers at night, Jerome prayed for the homeless, the sick, and anyone who was going through some sort of challenge in life. One year he drew a picture depicting a Christmas scene. It wasn't until I saw the picture that I realized God had granted Jerome the talent of drawing. At first, I thought he had traced the picture, but I never would have crushed his spirit by accusing him of tracing the image. Instead I asked, "Jerome, can you draw Mommy another picture like this?"

J.B.'s

Youthful Artworks

Call: (213) 674-4185
P.O. Box 29212
L.A., CA 90029

He looked straight into my eyes with great excitement, "Yes, Mommy, I can!"

I watched with great interest as his little fingers began to draw on the paper. I was amazed and delighted beyond belief when I witnessed his gift in action. Jerome had never taken any professional classes, and I realized my son had a God-given talent. As his parent, I was responsible for helping to nurture what God had placed inside Jerome. From then on, I set out purchasing all types of art supplies for him. Jerome even sold pictures he drew to neighbors. I had business cards printed with "Jerome's Youthful Artworks," on them. and we gave the cards to potential customers. Jerome was only ten years old at the time.

Eventually, I enrolled Jerome in an art program at one of the colleges in Los Angeles. He won several art contests, and I couldn't have been prouder. I remember a specific art contest in Venice Beach where Jerome drew the Statue of Liberty. His work won first place. After Jerome graduated from high school, he seemed to put the art interest aside and wanted to pursue a career in marketing.

As I sat at the desk of the United States Marine Corps recruiter's office in Virginia Beach, after Jerome enlisted, I wondered what my son had signed himself up for. Jerome's decision changed the entire course of his life and our family forever. As the recruiter sold the idea to me, I let my guard down a little and wondered if the Marines would give Jerome more direction in life.

Looking back though, I can't help but wonder: What on earth was I thinking? Jerome became the property of The United States Marine Corps when he signed his paperwork on July 31, 2002. He reported to boot camp on October 15, 2002, at the United States Marine Corps Recruit Depot in Parris Island, South Carolina. He signed over eight years of his life—four years active and four years inactive—to the Marines.

When I finally boarded the flight back to Los Angeles, I had one less child with me. How does that happen? How do you go on a family vacation, and your son doesn't return home with you? It was so hard to board the plane and waving good-bye to Jerome, my sister, and her sons.

The five-hour flight felt like the longest I had ever endured. I wondered if I would ever wake up from my bad dream. How had I allowed such madness to take place? I looked at the empty seat Jerome should have been in. It dawned on me that he really was in Virginia Beach, and was property of the Marines.

Without Jerome with us, it felt strange to be home in Los Angeles. I went to Jerome's office and informed his boss that Jerome joined the Marines while we were on vacation, and that I was there to get his last paycheck, as well as any personal belongings Jerome had left at the office. I told Jerome's boss I would come back, if necessary, to ensure all loose ends with Human Resources were tied up.

I left my mom's home to move into an apartment when I was eighteen years old. At sixty-three, the only thing I remember is that my mother and I cried a river of tears that night I decided to move out. Leaving the nest that day had been terrifying for me. Mom and I eventually cleaned es up and started laughing. We realized it was not the end of the world for me to move out. We planned to speak often on the phone.

I knew my son was not coming back any time soon. I stood in his bedroom and looked around at all his personal belongings. I stood in a daze, thoughts running through my head of my son returning home. There are some moments in life, when life as you knew it would never be the same again (and that's forever, a re-write in front of your eyes).

The thought of an extra bedroom did not sound too bad. I could finally move my office out of my bedroom. I could stop working late in my bedroom. I used the room to set up an altar to have my private talks with God. I did not realize at the time how much I would need that prayer altar. I could relate to the monks who went off to secluded areas to isolate themselves from the world. My God would take me away from harsh moments of reality.

My altar place gave me space to cry as many tears as I wanted. Some days, I sat in silence. But every day I laid at the feet of God. I was free to mourn and groan to God, expressing my deepest pain. The altar was a place of solitude and a safe refuge when I became frightened because I hadn't heard from Jerome.

I missed Jerome a lot and frequently called him to check in. There were times I wondered if Jerome shouldn't have left. In those times, though, I would tell myself that everything would be okay. Jerome would be okay.

I never realized the differences in the military branches prior to Jerome joining; however, I quickly learned. The Marines are trained to kill. They are the first to go in and seize a territory. When Marines return home, they are not fully equipped to transition back into every day, civilian life. I realize since the time when my son returned from Iraq there is more support for our military families, however, they are not receiving the level of support that is needed for soldiers and their families. Spouses, children, and extended family members also need to be taught a basic understanding of what their loved ones go through when they return home from war. Knowing what signs to look for, what triggers can set soldiers off, and how to navigate through PTSD and other mental illnesses is important. Families must learn how to communicate with their soldiers in a new language. They are not the same as they were prior to military training, deployments, and all that is part of the military culture.

Jerome had to sign several, legal documents during his enlistment. The first was the "Enlistment Document Armed Forces of the United States," which included an eight-year commitment and a starting salary of $1,022.70 per month (comparable to a grade E-1, first pay grade for a Marine -Private as a title). Jerome had to fill out a power of attorney (POA) form, on which he listed me as his POA. That meant I was to manage and conduct all his affairs in his name and on his behalf. Two other documents included "Restrictions on Personal Conduct in the Armed Forces," and a "Certificate and Acceptance and Confirmation of Enlistment."

LIFE LESSON THREE

One act in life can change the entire trajectory of your life,
and everyone associated with you.
by Million Heir-Williams

Chapter 4
BOOT CAMP EXPERIENCE

J erome went to boot camp with his cousin, Ramel, because Jerome and Ramel were in the "Delayed Entry Program." They had both been in pre-training for six months before they entered boot camp. Chris, Jerome's other cousin, left on time. So, he had already graduated from boot camp by the time Jerome and Ramel got there.

During pre-training, the recruiter taught Jerome and Ramel about the different ranks, general orders of the Marine Corps, and the Marine Corps hymn. The recruiter informed Jerome and Ramel that when they arrived at boot camp, the drill instructors would call on the recruits to find out if they knew the information. None of the recruits wanted to experience the embarrassment that came with a drill instructor signaling him or her out of the crowd.

The recruiter drove Jerome and Ramel to the Military Entrance Processing Station (MEPS). They boarded the USMC bus to Parris, NC. As the bus pulled up, drill instructors got on the bus and yelled orders at the top of their lungs.

Once Jerome was off the bus, the soldiers were told to walk toward the yellow footprints at a 45-degree angle and stand on them. Then, the drill instructor went over the Uniform Code of Military Justice. The United States "Congress shall have the power to make rules for the government and regulations of the land and naval forces" (US Constitution Art. 1 Sec. 8).

Jerome went through processing, where he was allowed to make one phone call and let me know he arrived. Jerome had to follow a specific script for the phone call, too. Next, he had to give up all his personal articles, including the clothes on his back and his cell phone. Jerome also had to get a haircut. Before he left for boot camp, Jerome was told to bring his driver's license, social security card, and banking information. He was not to bring anything else with him. Everything he needed would be issued by the Marines.

My husband has shared stories of how different the Marine Corps culture was in the seventies. He was told, "If the Marine Corps wanted you to have a wife, they would issue you one." So, you see, the culture has changed quite a bit.

Jerome told us one story about his rack mate. He told Jerome he grew up in a racist family, but that he was glad to meet Jerome and have the chance to get to know him because it gave him a different perspective of African-Americans. Jerome became rather good friends with his rack mate during boot camp training.

I never thought about how the Marines could bring so many different ethnicities and cultures together. Once you get into a firefight together, all that racism goes out the window.

My husband told me when he was a drill instructor, there was no centralized academic training section. So, drill instructors were assigned to teach Marine Corps Customs & Courtesy (education). As the second hat, my husband was assigned to teach that course. The curriculum did not include the history of the Montford Point Marines. The centralized academic section of boot camp at Parris Island was created in the 1980s. To this day, it is my personal assumption that the Montford Point Marines are still not included.

At one point, Jerome realized he was the second oldest out of his fellow recruits. The younger recruits looked up to him like he was a big brother.

I asked Jerome how he liked the food. He said it was good, but had a specified time to finish his meals. The cafeteria was called the mess or chow hall, and the food was called chow. If a Marine was still eating by the specified end time, he or she had to throw food out and get back to orders. Socializing was not allowed in the chow hall. Prior to entering the chow hall, soldiers' weapon had to be placed outside. One Marine was left on duty to watch the weapons.

During boot camp, Jerome shared that he dealt with drill instructors who were very hard on him, but they were hard on everyone, so Jerome didn't take it personally. Anytime recruits responded to drill instructors, they had to say, "Aye, Aye Sir." The recruits were micromanaged. Everyone took a shower in the evening and went to bed at 2100 (9:00 pm). Then, the Marines had to get up at 0400 (4:00 pm), and stand at attention in front of their racks. The recruits then received the command to count off, which meant everyone had to be accounted for. Then, the recruits received orders to make their racks. Once the racks were made, the recruits got back in line to receive their next command, which was to obtain items from their footlockers and get their shaving kits. Once the recruits got their shaving kits and locked their footlockers, they received the command to face right or left, depending on what side of the squad bay they were on, and then received the command, "Forward march." The Marines marched into the head, or bathroom.

Once the recruits were finished, they got back in line and marched back to their assigned place in front of their racks. The last thing the recruits did in the morning was to secure their shaving kits and footlockers and get dressed. There was an understanding that Marines had to quickly learn and adapt to orders in order to survive. It taught them to be prepared for something bigger than themselves, including deployment and, ultimately, war.

On Friday evenings, for approximately thirty minutes, the Senior Drill Instructor would allow recruits to ask general questions, which fostered morale for the group. Jerome said one of the recruits asked a question about God and the Senior Drill instructor told the group that he was probably the most religious person the recruits would ever meet.

Additionally, the Senior Drill instructor had nicknames for each recruit. Jerome's nickname was DooDoo Brown. At first, Jerome was disturbed about the name, but as time went by, he got used to it and never gave it any more thought. The Senior Drill Instructor had strange nicknames for all the recruits, so it was standard practice.

Jerome got sick— minor cold flu symptoms—a few times while at boot camp. He was sent to the Navy Corpsman who was called "Doc." Jerome never experienced any other type of illnesses during his time in boot camp, which was a blessing.

Jerome told us about a situation when one of the recruits started acting abnormal and jumped on other recruits' racks and cut his wrist with a razor. The recruit was immediately taken away and did not come back. Some recruits do not always make it to boot camp graduation. Training to become a Marine can be one of the hardest mental, and physical, requirements a person may endure in life.

Two weeks prior to graduation, the recruits received word from Marine Corps headquarters, which was located in Washington, DC, about what duty station and what job assignment they got. The Armed Services Vocational Aptitude Battery (ASVAB) scores determined the soldiers' Military Occupational Specialty Code (MOS). During his first month of boot camp, Jerome attended school for physical fitness. His second month he practiced drill maneuvers, and in his third month he practiced mental and physical fitness together.

The classes were highly structured and performance based. Classes were Monday through Friday and drill took place on Saturdays, as well as some down time. On Sundays, the soldiers could attend church.

Jerome was assigned to Camp Lejeune, which was close to where I lived at the time. He attended School of Infantry (SOI) for seven weeks, which consisted of Marine Combat Training (MCT) at Camp Geiger, in North Carolina.

As I spoke with Jerome about his boot camp experience, he told me there were things he did physically that he never thought he could do. As a result, it boosted his confidence quite a bit. The "Crucible" is the final exam for boot camp, which is fifty-four hours of nonstop activity out in the woods that includes running, climbing a wall, executing mock combat, rope climbing, more than forty-five miles of marching, carrying your partner for half a mile, standing in a gas chamber for eight minutes, and training in cold and hot weather. Jerome said that knowing there was an end date to the process was the greatest motivator. He knew the instructors had a lot of confidence in him during that final exam.

Despite the grueling training, Jerome's hardest time in boot camp was after church each Sunday, when he returned to duty, there was a sense of his freedom taken away. Jerome felt free during praise and worship.

I sent Jerome a lot of letters while he was in boot camp. The first letter I wrote was dated October 28, 2002 (copy in the Appendix). It was the first time in life that I had a chance to write my son letters. Several years after Jerome was discharged from the military, we sat and read through the letters I wrote to him. I genuinely enjoyed the experience. We sat and read through sixteen letters I sent while he was at boot camp.

After the longest time, I got a phone call from Jerome that he was going to graduate from boot camp. I let out a heavy sigh of relief.

I flew into Virginia Beach, and my sister and I drove to Parris Island, South Carolina, to watch our Marines graduate. It was the first time in my life that I witnessed a boot camp graduation. So many families were there to support their children, and all the graduates looked the same. It was a picture-perfect sea of Marines. There were thousands of Marines everywhere you looked. I did not know how I was supposed to distinguish Jerome from the others.

When we finally found Jerome, because of this great accomplishment of becoming a Marine, he had a very proud look on his face and his chest was as big as the Grand Canyon. My son looked stunning in his uniform. That moment in life will always be near and dear to my heart. My son was a Marine. I shed so many tears both during and after the ceremony. I was overwhelmed with pride. All the families shared a sense of unity and patronage to the United States. Once the ceremony ended, my sister and I headed back to Virginia Beach.

LIFE LESSON FOUR

Until we are pushed to the limits;
we never know who we really are in life!
by Million Heir-Williams

Chapter 5
PRE-DEPLOYMENT

The phone rang at six in the morning on February 23, 2004. When I answered, I heard my son crying. Ordinarily, Jerome should have been reporting for duty on a Monday morning, so it worried me to hear him crying on the phone. Jerome already knew his late arrival was going to be a problem with his command.

Then, I heard an older woman's voice. "I have your baby. He is fine, I have him," she said. "He had a flat tire. Do you know where Piney Green Road is located?"

"Not at all," I replied, "but I will find it. I will be right there."

Stephen, who would become my husband in the future, and I had just met two weeks ago—when I moved to North Carolina. He was the only person I knew to call. I had no idea how he would react to my desperate call. I also realized Stephen was probably getting ready for work. I held my breath as the phone rang. Before I could even finish relaying everything, Stephen said, "I'm on my way." My sigh of relief was like a deep release in the abyss. Peace filled my entire being.

Stephen picked me up and drove me to Piney Green Road to rescue Jerome. I prayed the whole way there. After twenty minutes, we arrived in front of a diner. I ran inside and found Jerome, who was still crying. I hugged him tight. An older, African-American woman introduced herself as Karen Warner. I thanked her multiple times for being there for my son. She was Jerome's angel. Stephen, Karen, and I stood in a circle and prayed for Jerome.

Karen remained in our lives until the Lord called her home. She was there when Jerome got orders to deploy to Iraq, and she was with us when he returned home. I was incredibly grateful for Karen's part in our lives during that significant period.

Several months passed, and Stephen and I got married. I have always held a core belief that if I can't depend on someone at the lowest point of my life, then I don't need that person when life is good. God showed me who Stephen truly was in a matter of two weeks. I am still grateful for my husband to this day. He is a man of great courage and character. Believe me, ladies, I protect my gates at all costs, and do not mind telling anyone. Hopefully, you do the same for your gates. All I can tell you is: Let God bring the right person to you, and it will be right.

Several days after we got married Jerome's platoon leader called and asked if I had seen Jerome. He had not reported for duty. Later that day I received a late-night call from my daughter, Candis, around one in the morning. She sounded unsettled.

"Candis, what is the problem?" I asked.

"Mom, did you get the text from Jerome?" She asked. "Something is wrong with him."

"No," I replied. "I didn't realize he sent me a text."

I was stunned as I read what he wrote. The text was very jumbled, and I thought he was hallucinating or on something. The first text said:

If you want to find your son, he is with the hawk on the street next to the church

The next text said:

I feel and smell the air. Still, it is not the same

The third text said:

I love the Lord, and he will help me

The fourth text said:

I'm okay baby girl

(Jerome always referred to his sister as "Baby girl")

The fifth text said:

I just gotta sort this out but really as physically, I'm okay—health is good

The last text said:

Got a place to rest just the mind is off a little.

Stephen woke up while I was still on the phone with Candis. As soon as I got off the phone, I told Stephen we needed to find Jerome.

"Where is he?" Stephen asked.

"I don't know," I said. "God does, and that is enough for me."

We got dressed left the house around one-thirty. We had no idea where to start, but I knew I was not returning home without my son. I turned to God and prayed one of the most ferocious prayers I ever declared on behalf of my son.

When you come to a fork in the road and must tap into the central intelligence of God, you must push through your emotions or you won't be able to hear the Holy Spirit's directions. As Stephen drove, I went back to Jerome's text to decode it. I felt like I was investigating a case, and every detail I had needed to be broken down. He had mentioned he was with the hawk on the street next to the church. There was a small church we had taken Jerome to once, and I thought we might find his car on that street. I had a flashlight so we could see down driveways, too. It took us about fifteen minutes, but we spotted his white Chevy blazer.

I cannot express the relief, gratitude, and the overwhelming emotions that ran through me. Just as soon as peace ran through me, I felt dread. In what state would I find my son? I prayed Jerome had not overdosed on drugs or anything like that. I was not emotionally or mentally prepared. I had to be strong and rely on my faith.

Jerome's car was parked near a trailer, so we knew he had to be in there. I was glad it was not an apartment complex. We wouldn't have known which door to knock on. Stephen and I took a few minutes to gather ourselves. Then, Stephen knocked on the door. We heard Jerome ask, "Who is it?"

"Your mom and dad. Open the door!"

Jerome opened the door. The look on his face was priceless.

"Mom, how did you find me?"

"You can't hide from God, and He won't let you hide from me."

Jerome's demeanor was way off, and I could tell he was on drugs and alcohol. As I looked around the inside of the trailer, I saw alcohol on the table, and things were out of place. A young woman appeared. She said her name was Mary. She had a pleasant demeanor. I was grateful it was not a house full of people with wild things going on.

We talked with Jerome for a while before I asked how long was he going to remain on unauthorized absence?

"Mom, I'll go back in a couple of days."

"We need you back at the house tomorrow," I said. "We can help you figure things out. You can't stay in this condition and hope to get better."

Jerome agreed and assured me he would be home sometime the next day. Stephen and I hugged him and went back home.

Jerome returned home the next day, and we were able to get him to return to duty the day after that.

Since it was Jerome's first infraction, his authorities told him not to do it again. They did place him on restriction for two weeks. He had to report to his staff sergeant on command post every hour on the hour until he went to sleep. He always had to stay in uniform and was told what time he could go to bed, and what time he could eat. Each of his activities were documented and overseen by the staff sergeant. Prior to him being on restriction Jerome drank excessively and hung out at clubs, which created a very toxic lifestyle.

Jerome got a speeding ticket on August 22, 2004, and then he didn't show up for court. I got involved because his Battery Commander called and informed me. Jerome was supposed to deploy the next month. I made phone calls on Jerome's behalf and had his Gunnery Sergeant fax the original deployment order to the legal assistant of the District Attorney and to me. The assistant was able to get the court date changed to when he returned from deployment. Jerome's new court date was for May 3, 2005, in Kinston, North Carolina.

Jerome accumulated three unauthorized absences, which was not favorable in the Marines. As a result of these three infractions, Jerome received nonjudicial punishment, was placed on restriction, and served a month in the brig, which is military jail time. He was also demoted from Lance Corporal to Private First Class, and then to Private, which is the rank assigned to Marines when they first enlist. Each of those demotions lowered his pay scale. Along with the demotion, Jerome's chain of command inventoried his room to ensure there was nothing Jerome shouldn't have in his barracks. Ultimately, Jerome's negative actions got him an "other than honorable" discharge from the Marine Corps. As stated by the Veterans Administration's (VA's) policy, a veteran has to receive an "honorable" or "other than honorable" discharge in order to receive benefits from the VA. Unauthorized Absence, Missing in Action is known as an unpardonable sin in the Marines. The United States Marine Corps could care less why Jerome had unauthorized absences. The fact that he *had* those absences was more than enough for the Marine Corps. As a mother, I was more concerned with *why* Jerome had failed to show up so many times. I started my journey which was getting my son the desperate medical help he needed since he was not in his right mind; and no one could stop my mission.

Jerome explained to me that he did not want to go to get up early. He did not want to go to work anymore, and he did not want to be a Marine. While Jerome was on restriction, he said "Mom, I see things and receive subliminal messages." My husband and I informed Jerome's staff sergeant about what Jerome told us, and I remember asking him, "Do you think Jerome has PTSD?" The staff sergeant looked at me as if I were crazy. I knew I had to go beyond what was occurring and fight for my son's rights and get senior leadership involved in the process to ensure he was taken care from a medical perspective. When we realized the staff sergeant was clueless to the term PTSD, I reported the staff sergeant's reaction regarding the question of PTSD. As soon as I reported this information the senior leadership Jerome was admitted to the Naval Hospital for evaluation. Jerome had mentally disconnected from the military and experienced a lot of anxiety about military life in general.

To this day, I do not think Jerome was military material from the beginning. Even my husband and I had a conversation about it. I asked Stephen, "Doesn't the military know from the beginning who is made for that type of endurance?" He said that drill sergeants would place bets on who would not make the platoon. Personally, I think if the leaders know someone is not cut out for military life, an alternate discharge should exist. Stephen had an entire career as a Marine, so if anyone knew who was able to carry the Marine torch, it was him.

LIFE LESSON FIVE

We never know what just might push us over the edge,
by Million Heir-Williams

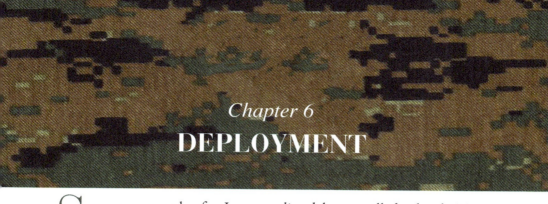

Chapter 6
DEPLOYMENT

Seventeen months after Jerome enlisted, he was called to battle. The Colonel announced the entire battalion would be deployed. The announcement stirred up real nervousness and anxiety in Jerome.

I can't explain what went through my mind when Jerome told me he had to deploy. I could tell Jerome had a lot of uncertainty, but he wasn't the only one experiencing anxiety, panic, and doubt. I struggled with apprehension and had several emotional breakdowns. When Jerome first enlisted, I thought he would cruise through his four years and then he would be home.

Now, I tell everyone war changes the inside of a person's soul. A soldier's exposure to war lives on inside them well past their time on the battlefield. Upon soldiers' return to the states, they then have to take on the mental "warzone" that veterans and their families frequently experience. Family members, if they haven't served in the armed forces, can be clueless about what soldiers must deal with when they return home.

I have always said that I am grateful to God that Jerome was not married and did not have children while he went through the darkest hours of his life. No wife, husband, or child should suffer behind the closed doors of their homes because of the sacrifice their loved ones made for our freedom. Families across the United States suffer in silence because of PTSD. Family members are not trained and do not have the expertise to deal with the emotions and mental disorders soldiers may return home with.

My heart goes out to the millions of American families having to deal with this secret in their family. I know how it creates feelings of hopelessness, loneliness, and defeat.

In October 2002, the United States Congress permitted President George W. Bush to use military force against Iraq if he felt the need. President George W. Bush started the war on Iraq on March 20, 2003.

Jerome enlisted in the Marines during the summer of 2002. Seventeen months after Jerome joined the Marines, the United States was in active war. He was called to serve the country in the battle against Iraq on September 7, 2004. He was slated to return home from war on April 7, 2005. His original orders said, "Authorize government vehicle from CLNC (Camp Lejeune, North Carolina) to Cherry Point, North Carolina and return, authorize government air from Cherry Point, North Carolina to Kuwait and return."

I still remember the day we drove to Camp Lejeune to see Jerome and the other Marines off.

So many families were gathered around and hugging their loved ones. Tears rolled down all of our faces, knowing our loved ones were headed off to war in a foreign land.

I told Jerome to make sure he emailed me as soon as he got to his assignment. I made Jerome promise that he would always respond back to me as much as he was allowed. Most of my correspondence with Jerome was by email, but I wrote him three physical letters during his deployment. Other family members also wrote to him.

As the days went by, I thought I would feel relieved. I can recall it took quite some time for our new "normal" to settle in. I found myself continuously praying for Jerome. I sought the most powerful intercessory prayer partners I knew and we all prayed nonstop for him.

In a specific moment, I received a vision of Jerome. He was balled up in a fetal position and he had been overcome by fear. I physically felt the fear crawling around Jerome and taking over. I fasted and prayed at that point. I am grateful to God that I was equipped with my faith to go through that process. It took a lot of mental courage, tenacity, and powerful prayers to get Jerome and our family through that time in our lives. No one in a family is immune to the feelings that come with a loved one being away at war. Until I experienced Jerome away at war, I had no idea of the deep emotions that plague you the entire time. Before our family's experience, I had been clueless about what military families dealt with.

It should be a federal mandate that anytime a soldier is deployed, the family members must complete a program that helps them understand the potential changes that may arise when their loved ones return from war. It is critical to know the signs of PTSD and understand what soldiers deal with. Some of the mass killers across America have been perpetrated by military experience. Having a program in place that teaches family members how to look for unusual signs in their loved ones returning from deployment will not prevent all innocent deaths, but I think it is a step in the right direction for our country to engage upon.

Take a moment to think about what America would look like if soldiers did not sacrifice everything to protect us. When you see or speak with a veteran, always thank them for the sacrifice he or she made. There are so many unsung heroes in our communities.

If you are a veteran reading this book, I am honored to know you risked your life for me and hundreds of millions of others to allow us the freedoms we take for granted every day. Please forgive us for our insensitivities as it relates to you and the importance of your service to this country.

While I lived in Jacksonville, North Carolina, I recognized that the community took many opportunities to acknowledge our veterans. Onslow County has provided that platform for our veterans all along.

During his time in the Marines, Jerome deployed to:
- Camp Fuji, Japan
- Fort Magsaysay, Philippines
- Marine Combat Training;
- Motor Transportation School
- The Fleet
- Camp Lejeune, North Carolina

- Okinawa, Japan
- Palayan, Nueva Ecija, Philippines
- Camp Fuji, Japan
- Camp Abidjan, Kuwait,
- Abu Ghraib, Iraq (Jerome guarded this prison while in Iraq).

When Jerome first arrived in Japan, he immediately experienced culture shock. It took Jerome about six months to get used to a new way of life in Japan. Each day, Jerome inspected vehicles for damage and filled out trip tickets.

The culture and language of Japan stood out most to Jerome. He got in trouble a few times for staying out past the curfew. All Marines had to sign in when they returned to the barracks. Marines were supposed to be back on base by 11:30 every night. If Marines returned later than curfew, they were punished with extra workouts or their privileges to leave base were revoked. Any Marine who broke curfew also had to stay in the barracks that the Non-Commissioned Officer monitored. For safety reasons, Marines were always told to leave the base as a pair.

Jerome never stayed off base at night. Higher ranking officials were able to stay out later. Jerome's worst experience happened when he came back from field operations. His Staff Sergeant was waiting for him in front of the barracks. Jerome had forgotten his backpack in the field and had gone to retrieve it. Jerome found out from other Marines that the Sergeant had his gear. Not too long after Jerome got to his room, the Sergeant started hazing him. Initially, Jerome was told to stay in his room for two days and do push-ups. Jerome mentioned the hazing to someone else and it got back to the Sergeant. As a result of the Sergeant being told Jerome knew he was about to haze him the Sergeant returned Jerome's backpack. Therefore, the Sergeant let Jerome go because he would have gotten in trouble for hazing him.

Listed below are emails from Jerome and myself while he was deployed.

To: Jerome
From: Mom
Date: September 10, 2004 at 10:02 a.m.
Hello Champion!
I thank GOD for being my son. You see Jerome, like GOD I see the finished product in you. Standing strong in GOD in the things he has called before you were ever formed in my womb. GOD has a definite plan for your life, and you will walk into what GOD has already pre-ordained for your life, in spite of you. You see son, Jesus has already paid your debt for the sins you have committed and the ones you will commit. There are so many people that LOVE you Sooo oooooooooooooooooooooooooooooooooooooooooooooo much! There are so many prayers at the heart of GOD on your behalf, it's wonderful. You will be the Man of GOD he has called you to be. So, go with GOD, you can't lose!!!!!!!

I LOVE YOU SON!
MOM FOREVER

From: Jerome (first email from Jerome during deployment)
To: Mom
Date: September 15, 2004
Touch down your son has made it. I'm here and you don't have anything to worry about because GOD is and has kept me safe. It's is a real good feeling to know that someone can have a family as supportive as mine. I love both of you mom and dad. I will keep you posted on my walk with GOD and my mental/physical health. I can't tell you other things that are going on, but I am pretty sure dad can fill you in Mother about why not.
Love you Mom

From: Mom
To: Champion
Date: September16, 2004
Hi Champion, These are the emails I receive each week from a brother in the Lord. His name is Mark, he is out of L.A. He has a ministry on-line called Morning Meditations I'll forward them to you from time to time. You must read this one I've forwarded to you. Share with some of your comrades. GOD Bless The Entire Echo Battery Unit!!!! We Love you and Will Continue to Keep You in Our Prayers! LOVE MOM

From: Mom
To: Jerome
Date: September 16, 2004 at 3:17 a.m.
Make My Day!
The tears of JOY have flowed from my eyes, to hear from you. How often are you able to get to the computer to respond to emails? I thank GOD for technology, to know that I can hear from you in this way as opposed to the mail that will take so long to get to you. Of course I will still send you letters in the mail. I sent Candis and Michael your address as well as your email address. I'll make sure that Saeed and Andre get your email address, and your Dad.
I LOVE YOU SON & I'M VERY PROUD OF YOU ... MY CHAMPION!!!

From: Mom
To: Jerome
Date: September 20, 2004 at 1:28 a.m.
Oh son, Make me scream with goodness!!! Did you get Stephen's email? There was a prophetic word that came Saturday here at the house regarding you for me; GOD

has your son right in the palm of his hand. I am to remain in peace with your entire trip, because GOD has you so locked in. All I could do is cry tears of Joy once again. I love you son, as The Father loved his son Jesus. Can't wait until you return, but I guess I will, didn't have a choice, huh? Stay strong, be encouraged!!! Grandma, sends a shout out to you. Love ya ... 4-ever and ever ... Make sure you answer Stephen's email.

From: Champion
To: Mom
Date: September 25, 2004
THANK YOU MOTHER You are part of my motivation. You and dad have done more for me than any other person has ever done for me and for that I am grateful. I have been praying for my chain of command and for my family. No matter how far away you are from me GOD and my family will always be here I can feel the prayers going forth. Thank you for those powerful prayers you have been praying especially the ones in tongues they are very powerful.
LOVE your son # 1 CHAMPION

From: Mom
To: Jerome
Date: October 6, 2004 at 7:32 a.m.
Jerome,
I just love you soooooooooooooooooooooooooooooo much son! I am so at peace with you, the Lord is truly sustaining you and keeping you and me, while you're there. I look forward to you sharing once you get back, all that GOD has done through you. Well, actually I am witnessing through your writings. Stay connected to the Lord at all times. He said he will never leave you, nor forsake you.

P.S. David said to tell you, He has cleaned his room, don't get him in trouble! ha! ha!

From: Jerome
To: Mom
Date: October 6, 2004
Hey MOM
How are you doing as for me doing what I gotta do. I know it's been a while since I last wrote to you but sometimes this job really gets busy. Anyway, I miss you and the family very much before I go to bed at night I pray the angels and the blood of Jesus are encamped around you and dad. If you get a chance mother can you send me a daily scripture reading. Something small that I can keep on me when I go about the day. It is still very hot at times over here but I'm managing. It should be getting very cooler soon. Anyway Mother I'm going to go now, just writing you to let you know I am doing exceptionally well.
LOVE your champion JEROME
P.S. Tell DAVID to clean his room

From: Mom
To: Jerome
Date: October 6, 2004
Oh, My Champion,
You just don't understand how blessed your Mother really is by hearing from you as often as you respond. Don't get me used to something and then pull it away. So you better keep up the good work!!! By the way, have you responded to Sudie's email yet or Stephen? Make sure you email them. Karen keeps asking about her Jeremy. She needs to hear from you ASAP!!! Oh, Mom and MaryBeth are heading for Wilmington today. The rap group Outkast is doing a

movie. We will be in a scene. Aunt Michele's girlfriend's son knows the group, and he is working with them on the movie. This family is really headed for some big things. Watch out, Champion, you might see us on the big screen over in Iraq. (Ha! Ha!). Make sure you answer Candis's email also. How many people have emailed you? Please answer these questions when you respond next time. Well son, over and out Commander. I got my marching orders!!!

Who loves ya, baby? Ya Momma!

From: Jerome
To: Mom
Date: October 7, 2004
GOOD MORNING MOTHER
How are you doing well as for me I'm blessed. Happy to be alive and breathing. Happy about LIFE. There's a lot I know that he wants to do for me. Sometimes it takes other people for you realize that there is God inside all of us. I have also been reading TD JAKES again. I plan on reading a scripture when I wake up and before I lay my head on my pillow at night.

Your son is signing out now but I will write you later.
LOVE your son JEROME BROWN

From: Mom
To: Jerome
Date: October 18, 2004 at 3:25 a.m.
Hello Champion!
Where are you? Haven't heard from my son. Don't let me get on the next jet. You know your Mama. Laura, Brent and Gina was asking about you. Why haven't you written them lately? Alright now, don't let your Mama start acting up! And I do mean packing up. I'll have to send David overseas.

We'll be sending you a care package within the next couple of weeks. Is there anything specific you'd like? Waiting to hear from my Son!

From: Jerome
To: Mom
Date: October 29, 2004 at 9:59 a.m.
Hey Mother,
How's everything going with you and the family? Well as for me I'm just having a blast. I miss you Dad and Grandma very much Cpl Barben and Doc told me to tell you hi. Doc always asking about you and dad. A brotha still hittin the weights strong. Mom I feel the protection of Jesus all around me. I'm so thankful. I wrote Brent back and she sent me some pics. Beatrice wrote to me that Dolly had been going through some challenging situations. So I've also been praying for her. Mom if you can send me some of this stuff called AQUA VELVA. Dad knows what it is. Mom if you send me some calling cards I would really appreciate it too. Your son is in good health and I well.
LOVE your son "THE CHAMP"

From: Jerome
To: Mom
Date: November 3, 2004 at 4:36 p.m.
Hey Mom
How's it going? I miss you. It just started getting kinda chilly out here, mainly during the evening. I'm been keeping warm though. I just got an email yesterday from Kathy. She seems to be doing pretty good. I just wrote her back today. Matter fact speaking of writing back. Mom I wrote you not to long ago haven't heard from ah motha. Just writing you to let you know everything is fine health/mental/spiritual.

Anyway Mother write me back and let me know if you got the last email I sent out to you. Gotta go now but I will stay in touch with you dad and grandma.

LOVE your son the CHAMP

P.S. Send my love to everyone

From: Mom

To: Jerome

Date: November 4, 2004 at 4:20 a.m.

Hey Champ,

Pls. excuse the delay for responding so late. Our computer has been down for about a week. I will have someone to look at it this Saturday. I finally got the boxes to send you this week, so be on the lookout. I'm so very proud of you and your growth in the Lord!!! Yes we will send all your known request!

Love ya Mother

From: Mom

To: Jerome

Date: November 4, 2004 at 4:51 a.m.

Hello Champion!

The reason I'm able to email you is because I'm at a friend's home. She will look at the computer this Saturday. Therefore, I will be emailing kinda Mom to a son. You know your Mom isn't having this too long. Not being in touch with her homey! Give all the guys my love. Our prayers are with ya!!!

Love ya Momma!

From: Jerome

To: Mom

Date: November 14, 2004 at 4:52 p.m.

Hello Mother

It's your son the Champ how are you doing? Hey don't even answer that question because I know your doing just fine. How's Grandma doin? Tell her I said I love her very much. I've been keeping in touch Candis quite often. Candis just sent me some pics of our cousins. I had no idea Mary had a baby. Have you been in touch with Arnette? If you talk to her in the near future send her my love. Any way mom I'm living day to day and staying out of trouble. I've been praying for you and the family.

LOVE JEROME the CHAMP

I love you! I LOVE YOU!

From: Mom

To: Jerome

Date: November 15, 2004 at 1:50 p.m.

Hey Champ!

You Mom is back in computer business, FINALLY!! I'm answering my emails again. It is a blessing to be back in the mix. I truly miss corresponding with you, my brotha. Mom misses hearing from the Champ!. Everything is going so well. I thank GOD for his new mercies each and every day. Karen told me you spoke with her on-line. I am looking forward to that moment happening with us. Girl scout promise, your box will be mailed by the end of the week. I know, you want calling cards, what other items do you want?

gotta run, going to bible study. I love you.

From: Mom

To: Jerome

Date: November 24, 2004 at 4:38 a.m.

Top of the Morning to you Champ!

Well Mom finally has the computer back up and running. I had to take it back to the woman who had fixed it the first time. She had done a partial recovery on the system, but that still didn't suffice, so therefore I had to spend a day with her to fully recover the system. How is my No. 1 son, I pray GOD's favor and righteousness on you, his grace and mercy upon all the days of your life. I guess you are probably wondering what's up with your box I am sending you. Well, it goes a little something like this. The family is coming over for Thanksgiving, there are some things I'd like them to participate in, so just hold on a minute. I will send the box this Friday. Sorry about that Boo. I promise, ya. Give the crew my love and let them know our prayers constantly go out for you guys each and every day. Jerome, I miss ya boy David says Hi! And to tell you he cleaned his room. Ha! Ha! Ha!

From: Jerome
To: Mom
Date: November 30, 2004 at 7:27 a.m.
Hey Mother how you doing?
Fine I know. Im handling business out here in Iraq. Staying positive and motivated in my own way. I miss you guys and just know that I will be home soon. The time is really flying by out here. I'll Be home in like 4 months. I'm glad to know that the computer is back up and running. Mom I tried emailing Mr kingdom and it did not work. So if pops changed his email let me know. I wrote him a really long email. I'm in good contact with baby Thandis (Candis). I emailed her and Migelito when I get the chance. Anyway just writing to let you know that I miss you and love you.
LOVE, THE CHAMP
P.S. Tell Grandma I said that I miss her and love her.

P.S. Is she still watching her Westerns?
P.S. Tell pops I said OORAHHHHHHHH

From: Mom
To: Jerome
Date: December 3, 2004 at 4:40 p.m.
Hey Champ!
You won't believe who has the same birthdate as you. Your bonus grandmother Karen. I was sharing with her you may be home March 9. I was about to tell her that was your birthday, I could hardly get it out when she got all excited saying her Jeremy coming home on her birthday! So you know GOD will more than likely keep that date for a lot of reasons.
We love ya!!!!

From: Mom
To: Jerome
Date: December 22, 2004 at 5:47 a.m.
Dear Champ,
Let me know you're alright. We saw on the t.v. Mosul explosion. How far are you from that occurrence?

From: Jerome
To: Mom
Date: December 22, 2004 at 8:25 a.m.
Hello Mother,
How are you doing? I'm doing fine because I am covered by the blood of JESUS. No weapon formed against me shall prosper. The attack that happened in Mosul did happen several hours away
LOVE JEROME the champ

From: Mom
To: Jerome
Date: December 23, 2004 at 9:04 a.m.
Alright now Champ!
I just needed to hear from a brotha. I thank GOD for his divine protection over, around, under and through you! Keep the faith my son. GOD will never fail you Champ. He is in the blessing business. We love ya! Did you get the box we sent you? Love ya!!!!!!!

From: Mom
To: Jerome
Date: January 10, 2005 at 6:34 p.m.
Hey Champ,
I haven't heard from you. You know it's too long. Did you ever receive the box we mailed you? How are things going for you? I know the elections take place at the end of this month. What's the status where you are?
Give ya Mom & Dad a holla!!!

From: Jerome
To: Mom
Date: January 12, 2005 at 1:18 p.m.
Hey Mother
How you doin? I'm doing just blessed. I know you doing blessed. Forgive me for not writing sooner. It's crazy, I still have not received that package you sent me. If you put insurance on the package, please check to see if possibly it got lost or something. I know the elections are taking place but I'm not worried about the outcome. If I keep my mind focused on Christ he will keep me in the place that I need to be. I am a warrior, I've walked through this shadow of death but I fear no evil because LOVES me.

LOVE your CHAMP

P.S. health, mental, spiritual good

P.S. Tell Grandma and Big Poppa I love them and miss them

P.S. Be home sooner than you think, can't tell you when but I'll probably be home real soon

From: Jerome

To: Dad

Date: January 13, 2005

Hey Pops, How's everything let me guess, blessed. I know how you and Mom run the show. I know you guys are lifting me up in prayer. It is quite a blessing to have parents like you in my critical moment in development as a man, especially to be a man of Christ. I cannot think of a better way to grow as a man in Christ than to have a man to teach me such as yourself. God has still and always is good to me. I will probably be home sooner than you think. You might be expecting arrival from your son.

Love Jerome "THE CHAMP." Pls send Grandma my love and tell her I can't wait to watch some Westerns with her upon me return. Tell Mom I received the package you guys sent me, thank you so much!

From: Jerome

To: Mom

Date: January 26, 2005 at 1:38 p.m.

Hey Mother

How are you doing? As for your son I'm blessed in the LORD. I love and miss you very much. The video clip Every Eye was amazing. It almost brought tears to my eyes when I looked at it. That was a pretty powerful clip. I know it's been a while since I wrote but you know I will always be in touch with you. I'll be gone for a couple of days but when I

get back, I'll make sure to write you. I'm gonna go for now but I will talk to you and dad soon
LOVE "THE CHAMP"

From: Mom
To: Jerome
Date: January 28, 2005 at 12:41 p.m.
Hey Champion,
I am so glad you finally received the box we sent you. How soon will you be home? Will it be in February? We can hardly wait for the Champion's return. David is waiting too!

From: Mom
To: Jerome
Date: February 3, 2005 at 5:06 a.m.
Hi Champ,
A Mother needs to hear from her son! Let me know what's going on. When will you be home?

LIFE LESSON SIX

Prayers without ceasing and more prayers without ceasing!
by Million Heir-Williams

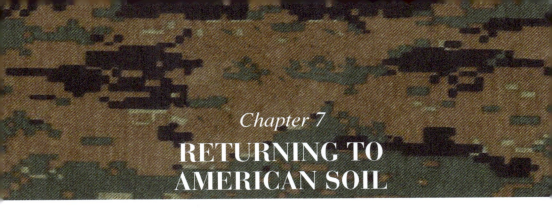

Chapter 7
RETURNING TO AMERICAN SOIL

When my son returned from Iraq, we were living in North Carolina. Stephen, Jerome, and I flew to California to celebrate Jerome's birthday and his safe return. Since Jerome had enlisted in the Marines while we were in Jacksonville, North Carolina, for a family reunion, Jerome hadn't been back to California in a few years. When he enlisted, the country wasn't at war either. When Jerome returned from Iraq, we planned the big celebration in California, so he could see his brother, sister, and friends. Approximately fifty people—both friends and family—met us at P.F. Changs in Manhattan Beach, California.

While at the restaurant, Diane Jones, one of my closest friends kept saying to me, "Something is wrong with my Jerome. He isn't the same when you look at him. There is a certain look in his eyes, that isn't Jerome."

The only thought on my mind at the time was that my son returned from war and still had all his body parts. I guess I was in denial because I did not want to believe something could be psychologically wrong with my son.

After Diane shared her thought with me, I walked over to Jerome and hugged him. I wanted to investigate how his eyes looked. A profound awakening came over me, and I felt like the rug had been pulled from under me because I saw the foreign look in my son's eyes. I could not let Jerome know that I knew something was wrong. He had a glossy stare beaming out of his eyes. It was very foreign to me. I got an eerie feeling of evilness; I had never seen that in my son. I was quite aware we needed to get him help when he got back to Camp Lejeune. It was imperative that he get the correct medical attention for whatever was going on with him. My prayer was that my Champion could hold on until we made it back to North Carolina.

By God's grace, we were able to get back home. Then our real journey began.

Once we retuned to North Carolina after celebrating Jerome's welcome home celebration; I hit the ground running to get Jerome the help he desperately needed. I found brick walls at every turn. At that time in 2006, PTSD did not receive a lot of attention. I was treated like a plague. No one on base wanted to pay attention to me. I went to

Jerome's Battery Commander, his Staff Sergeant, and even walked into the Commanding General's office—who was deployed at the time.

I had a real wild encounter with one of Jerome's staff sergeants. When he tried to dismiss me I said, "You haven't seen Iraq war yet. These stars, stripes, and other medals you have displayed on your uniform don't mean a thing to me." I was enraged at the lack of help and support from the base. I wrote a letter to the VA (copy of the letter in the Appendix), contacted my congressman, and sent a letter to the Naval Board of Corrections.

As I sat at the kitchen table with my husband one night, I said, "If none of these entities offer the assistance needed for Jerome, I will camp out on the steps of the White House until I have a conversation with President Bush and company!" I was willing to do whatever it took for my son and other veterans who felt silenced. How could a superpower country, such as the United States, ever allow such negligence to take place for our war heroes?

Off I went into the dark pit, not realizing what the journey entailed. From day one, though, I knew God had me. I was well guarded, equipped, anointed, appointed, directed, and divinely protected for my mission.

There were times when I'd be driving in the car with Jerome and he would say, "Mom, I still see the Humvee jeeps and six-ton trucks driving down the streets." He meant he saw those vehicles on the civilian roads in Jacksonville. Jerome would exhibit jerky movements in the car. He was always anxious, and constantly moved and turned to see what was over his shoulder. Jerome complained about nightmares as well.

Jerome could not sit still during the day. It was as if his mind were always racing and he could never slow down or turn off his thoughts. His energy level was always high. Sometimes I would suggest, "Champion, try and take a nap or sit down and relax." My words went into the abyss. Relaxing seemed like a foreign concept to him. Observing my son was tricky because he was someone I did not know. It felt like a stranger was in my home, and I was obligated to take care of him. I realized I had to be intentional and patient with Jerome. I started to understand Jerome's ways. It helped me navigate through this maze. I constantly prayed that God would keep my mind grounded.

I am grateful to God that I never let my fear overwhelm me. Sometimes I knew I was talking to other voices that took residence within Jerome. I, and several others, prayed that Jerome would fight through the spiritual warfare and that he would be delivered from his mental trauma. In one specific incident, I was up close to Jerome and looked deep into his eyes. "Don't let the bi-polar fool you," I said. "I am not the one because I'll give you some triple bi-polar." If I showed fear in in front of Jerome, I am sure that I would have been consumed as well.

There was one time Stephen, my sister, and I drove Jerome to Virginia Beach to visit a pastor. He was known to offer deliverance from demonic activity. Jerome sat in the back seat with my sister. All of a sudden, in an unrecognizable voice, Jerome said, "Mom, I know President Bush hired you, Dad and Aunt Michele to spy on me along with the CIA."

I began to frantically pray and did not let up. My sister joined me in prayer while Stephen continued to drive. Jerome stopped talking and finally chilled out for a while. Those types of episodes were a result of PTSD and other mental disorders Jerome suffered from.

We finally made it to Virginia Beach and were able to get Jerome to Pastor Sanders for prayer. Before long, we were back on the highway headed home. I utilized all my options to heal Jerome. I knew God would heal my son.

That is where my true faith came into play. I looked into the eyes of the adversary and spoke what the Lord said. I declared and proclaimed the will of God no matter how horrible the situation looked. We must trust God down to our core and know that He is at the center of it all. He will not fail us. The word of God says, "For we wrestle not against flesh and blood, but against principalities, against powers, against the rulers of the darkness of this world, against spiritual wickedness in high places" (Eph 6:12, Life Application Study Bible). Believe me. Those demonic fields were on a high level and had to be pulled down through prayer and fasting.

I wrote down certain events that took place with Jerome because there were so many to keep up with. Here are a few:

April 26, 2005
- Jerome called the Battery Commander and said, "I have car trouble, and it's going to cost two hundred dollars to get my car fixed. Once I get my car fixed, I'll return to base."

On May 2, 2005, at 3:00 p.m.
- Stephen and I sat in the Battery Commander's office. He informed us Jerome was UA since April 27, 2005. He also told us Jerome got a speeding ticket and was supposed to appear in court the next day. I told the Commander, "My husband and I have not heard from Jerome. We had no idea he was missing in action." I immediately went into the zone. I sat and listened in disbelief. I wondered if my son was dead or alive. Then I wondered where he was and what was going on. My eyes filled with tears. Thoughts and feelings of fear penetrated the depth of my inner soul. I wanted the Commander to check the barracks and see if Jerome was hiding in his closet. Then the reality hit that my son was missing in action, missing in life, and was missing from me. No one could tell me where my son was.

May 3, 2005 at 2:30 p.m.
- My husband and I went to the Jacksonville Police Department and filled out a missing person's report. That was the first time I had ever filled out a report like that.

May 4, 2005
- A detective of Jacksonville Police called me. He said he would be handling Jerome's missing person's case. He wanted to know if Jerome had GPS on his phone. I checked with his phone carrier, and he did not have a tracking system on his phone. I updated the detective with the information and informed him as soon as I heard from Jerome, I would call him.

May 13, 2005

- We met with Jerome's Battalion Commander. I asked, "What type of counseling do you offer returning Marines who are transitioning to American soil?" He replied, "We do warrior transitioning training in Kuwait for four to five days. The Chaplain is available if needed."

May 18, 2005

- Jerome comes home about 8:30 p.m. We were quite surprised. We took him to the Naval Hospital emergency department to get checked out. A doctor saw Jerome and diagnosed him as "Having difficulty adjusting in the military." The doctor said Jerome would be okay and was going to release him. I looked at the doctor. "I hope to God that something doesn't happen to my son, or that he doesn't hurt someone else or himself because you've released him. If that happens, I will go public with this information and tell the country, on national TV, about this situation." On top of all that, Jerome's blood pressure was 151/91 (extremely high reading for blood pressure) and his heart rate was 73. After my confrontation with the doctor, Jerome was admitted to the hospital. On May 18, 2005, at 11:09 p.m., Jerome was placed on the Alpha-Psych ward at the Naval Hospital, which was located at Camp Lejeune.

May 19, 2005

- I called the nurses' station to find out Jerome's status. "Jerome is stable, and the doctor will be in sometime today to speak with him," the nurse said.
- "Let my son know that I called to check on him and that I love him," I replied.

May 19, 2005

- Jerome's Battery Commander called and let me know Jerome would receive the best possible care.

May 23, 2005 at 11:49 a.m.

- Jerome was discharged from the hospital.

May 23, 2005 at 12:45 p.m.

- I went to see Jerome's First Sergeant. He was quite nasty and arrogant. He was quite disgusted that Jerome went UA. I was concerned about *why* Jerome went UA. The First Sergeant said, "Get your eyeballs off of me; you're acting like a four-year-old!" to Jerome. I was royally pissed off. I told the Sergeant I didn't appreciate the manner in which he addressed my son, and that I didn't care about his stripes. They meant nothing to me and I was not afraid of him.

May 25, 2005 at 7:30 a.m.

- Jerome had an appointment at Division Psychiatry. We realized we had to pay special attention to Jerome's behavior from that time forward. Serious negative changes in his behavior were going on with him. He appeared to be moving forward. I thought he was getting better. As time moved forward, though, so many things started to appear. We were headed toward a major show-down.

There is a phrase —Suck it up, Marine—that exists in the service. I cannot speak about the other military branches because I am unfamiliar. Still, I can talk about what I have personally witnessed and observed as the mother of a Marine. All that "sucking up" is far more damaging than we as Americans can understand. The results of sucking everything up can be so devastating to a person. Sucking it up creates a significant level of denial, which is very destructive to everyone, including family and friends.

There is a psychological term—cognitive dissonance—When you have two different internal mindsets and it presents an internal conflict.

LIFE LESSON # 7

When my son didn't have a voice, I became his voice!
by Million Heir-Williams

Chapter 8
FULL MENTAL BREAKDOWN

66 "Cognitive dissonance is an individual's psychological discomfort (dissonance) caused by two inconsistent thoughts", (King, 2013, p. 406).

This constant mental state of cognitive dissonance is not mentally healthy for anyone to be in this mindset at any time. It is a set-up for a mental breakdown if left untreated continuingly.

Jerome received an "other than honorable" discharge from the Marines, which meant they kicked him out without any medical or financial benefits. That didn't mean anything to me as his mother. My son's well-being was the only thing I was interested in. Six weeks after he was released from the military, Jerome had a significant mental breakdown. On July 10, 2006 Jerome moved through our house with a sudden outburst of profanity, aggression, rage, and anger. He stormed out of the house saying words I never heard Jerome say before.

Jerome was trained to kill and he was also deployed to Iraq for war. I understand the mission comes first and the welfare of the Marine comes second; however, the correct assistance must be provided to our troops upon their return to the states. If not, this is an equation waiting to breakdown.

We called the Jacksonville Police Department, and three officers were dispatched to our home. By the time they arrived, Jerome had calmed down. He sat on the curb in front of the house. After a female cop, who displayed some compassion, calmed Jerome down, we explained to her that Jerome had been released from the Marine Corps six weeks prior. The officer told me her husband had similar experiences when he returned home after several tours to Iraq. It was quite reassuring to know I was not alone.

We do not know what military family members face once they are back from war. It is all out warzone on the home front. We have not been trained to go into battle against mental disorders. I can't imagine small children having to see their mommies or daddies experience such a traumatic situation. If I had grandchildren at the time, I could not imagine them having to be exposed to such trauma. My heart goes out to the millions of American families who have not received the proper help they deserve.

Once the police officers explained the process for dealing with Jerome's outburst, they told us we had two choices. The first choice was that they could take Jerome in the police car. If they did that, Jerome would have to be handcuffed to protect himself and the officers. Immediately, I knew I did not want my son handcuffed. He was not a criminal, and he did not commit a crime. I knew he was mentally suffering.

The second choice was we could drive Jerome to the mental health center if we felt Jerome was calm enough. We would follow the police car to the center. Then, Jerome would be triaged by a doctor.

We chose to drive Jerome. We took him to the Onslow Carteret Crisis Unit. A nurse took Jerome back to the triage station. Stephen and I sat in the waiting room for what felt like forever. About five hours went by before the psychiatrist came to speak with us.

That experience was one of the most grueling and fearful situations I have ever gone through with one of my children. As the doctor described my son's medical condition, he spoke in a very flat, monotone voice. "Your son has PTSD, severe psychosis, paranoid schizophrenia, and is bi-polar," the psychiatrist said.

In that moment, I finally received medical proof that my son was severely unwell. Even though it didn't seem like it on the outside, that was the first step toward getting Jerome the treatment and financial compensation he needed due to the suffering he had endured while in combat. When Jerome was discharged from the military, I had to enroll him in Medicaid so he could receive medical assistance until the military recognized Jerome's need for treatment and took responsibility for his service-connected illness.

The psychiatrist demonstrated a lack of compassion as he communicated my son's diagnosis. How can any healthcare professional treat a family member as if he is reading a menu at a restaurant, as he is gave the list of mental disorders my son was diagnosed with? The doctor displayed insensitivity to what we were dealing with as a family during such a critical time in our lives. Some people in the medical field have absolutely no business serving people who are ill at the time of their suffering.

I stood frozen for a moment. Had I just heard what I thought I heard? I cannot imagine any parent being treated as we were, absolutely no regard or respect for our feelings in this delicate situation.

You must always have a voice for your loved ones when they are unable to represent themselves. I realize the human voice is an essential instrument God can give someone. Genesis 1:3 states, "And God said, 'Let there be light: and there was light.'" God's voice brought light into existence. I knew God chose me to serve as my son's voice in his dark days.

Jerome was admitted to the facility and they kept him overnight for observation. Stephen and I were emotionally drained on the drive home. I don't think we knew what to say after our experiences that night. Knowing when to stop talking speaks volumes. Part of me was relieved to know Jerome would finally get the help he needed. At the same time, my emotions spun out of control. I knew it was time to put the pedal to the metal. I had to contact the VA now that a medical professional had diagnosed my son's mental illnesses.

I went with Jerome to every therapist and doctor appointment he had. For the last six months of 2006, Jerome went to twelve therapy sessions. In 2007 he went to twenty-eight therapy appointments, and in 2008 he had twelve visits. I sat through every single appointment he had while Stephen and I lived in Jacksonville. I also went to Jerome's primary care appointments. Jerome took medication and was on different treatments, so his labs had to be monitored every six months, if not more frequently. Jerome tried many different medications and is still on some of them to this day. Doctor's tried valproic acid 250mg, Geodon 40mg, Symbyax 12/25mg, Zyprexa, Seroquel 200mg, aciphex 20mg, Invega 9mg, fluoxetine 20mg, selenium 2.5mg, guaifenesin/D-methorphan – P.O. 100/10mg, pseudo-ephedrine 30mg., zolpidem 10mg, aripiprazole 30mg, risperidone 4mg, divalproex 500mg, ziprasidone H.C.L. 20mg, benztropine mesylate 2mg, diphenhydramine 50mg, and Haloperidol 5mg.

Jerome has been on seventeen different medications, although not all at the same time. Over the years, Jerome's body has gone through a lot due to the medications in his system. That is a lot of medication for anyone to take. And believe me, there are side effects to all of it. That is why we have to be involved with our loved one's health and be an active part of their lives. We must be their voice.

Research the side effects of the drugs your loved one has been prescribed. They are powerful drugs that keep the mind chemically balanced, so your loved one will need your assistance along the way. In addition to monitoring your loved one's medication, you will need to know the definitions of their conditions.

Jerome was diagnosed with the following:

Post-traumatic Stress Disorder (PTSD): "It is an anxiety disorder that develops through exposure through a traumatic event that overwhelms the person's abilities to cope", (King, 2013, p. 452).

Bipolar Disorder: "A mood disorder characterized by extreme mood swings that include one or more episodes of mania, an overexcited, unrealistically optimistic state", (King, 2013, p. 457).

Psychosis: "Psychosis is characterized by an impaired relationship with reality. It's a symptom of serious mental disorders. People who are experiencing psychosis may have either hallucinations or delusions", (Carey, 2018, para. 1).

Schizophrenia: "Schizophrenia severe psychological disorder characterized by highly disorder thought process; individuals suffering from schizophrenia may be referred to as psychotic because they are so far removed from reality", (King, 2013, p. 468).

I kept copious notes along the way during Jerome's journey during his time in the military and when he was discharged:

July 15, 2006 at 10:00 a.m.

Jerome's therapist told us that if Jerome ever needed emergency care, a 24-hour crisis center was available.

July 17, 2006 at 9:30 a.m.

I took Jerome to the unemployment office. We ran into a friend who suggested we get Jerome involved with Vocational Rehabilitation. They would be able to help Jerome with employment.

July 16, 2006 at 11:00 a.m.

I called Congressman Walter B. Jones' veteran assistant. I informed him of Jerome's outburst on Saturday what conditions Jerome had been diagnosed with. He told me I needed to get a copy of the diagnoses and write a letter. I was told to address the letter to the congressman. They would assist with Jerome's status upgrade.

July 17, 2006 at 12:15 p.m.

I called the office of the N.C. Division of Vocational Rehab Services Dept. of Health and Human Services. I scheduled Jerome's appointment for August 6, 2006 at 9:30 a.m. I needed to bring Jerome's picture identification and his social security number.

July 24, 2006 at 1:30 p.m.

I scheduled an appointment with an attorney who specialized in overturning discharge orders. He informed me that I had done everything right in going about getting my son's discharge corrected.

Typically, he charged five thousand dollars to take a case like Jerome's. He informed me based on the letters I already wrote the VA and the additional documentation I showed him, that I should be able to get all of Jerome's medical and financial benefits, as well as back pay.

July 25, 2006 at 4:00 p.m.

I spoke with Congressman Walter B. Jones' office and provided an update on Jerome's information up to that point. The Congressman wanted to know if we were in touch with Disabled American Veterans (DAV), which was an organization that helped veterans and their families navigate through the system.

August 24, 2006 at 1:30 p.m.

I met with Congressman Walter B. Jones, and he was incredibly supportive and helpful. That is the reason I had to mention him in the memory section of the book. He truly supported the military while he served in public office. I was grateful to know such an honorable man of God.

September 11, 2006

I wrote a letter to the VA on behalf of my son. (A copy on the Appendix section of the book).

LIFE LESSON EIGHT

You cannot continue to hold in negative emotions;
They have a way of coming out,
one way or the other.
by Million Heir-Williams

Chapter 9
REFLECTING WHILE LOOKING
TO THE FUTURE

Mental illness is real and has its own set of variables for people to deal with in life. It is still a taboo subject, and it's still looked down upon in so many settings—especially in the military culture. Mental illness is displayed through alcoholism, drug abuse, promiscuity, and suicide.

We're not equipped or trained to see the triggers that are there all along, but they exist. With intervention, some suicides can be prevented. In some states, you can have someone involuntarily committed, should the need arise. When a person struggles with mental illness, they are the last ones to seek help. We have to look to our church and school leaders, lawmakers, neighbors, and businesses for support.

Mental illness has permeated the fabric of our nation for many generations. When I look at African American communities, specifically, we must have conversations to address the mental illness epidemic that plagues our communities. Prior generations kept silent. No wonder our culture suffers with so many dysfunctional abnormalities. I was fortunate that I did not grow up in a silent environment. My mother always allowed expression with respectful communication. It was safe for me to express myself and be comfortable at home.

As a free society, we must create a safe place for our service members, and others, to be able to ask for help. The stigma attached to mental illness must be removed or we will continue to pay a heavy price—the lives of our loved ones. We must face the invisible wounds of war and discover the unknown dynamic that our veterans struggle with daily.

LIFE LESSON NINE

I am that voice for the masses, be it written or verbal!
by Million Heir-Williams

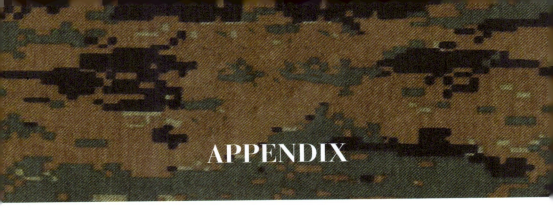

APPENDIX

A. References

B. The first letter I sent to Jerome at boot camp

C. Letter to Veterans' Administration

D. Jerome's Prayer of Deliverance

E. Glossary of Marine Corps Terms

F. Enlisted Rank Structure

G. Resource Directory

H. Statistics

Abhishek, P. (2017). Peace does not mean an absence of conflicts; differences will always be there Peace means solving these differences through peaceful means through dialogue education knowledge and through humane ways. Retrieved from http://mindfultibet. com/14-quotes-on-education-and-knowledge-by-his-holiness-dalai-lama/3-3/

Britannica. (2019). Buffalo soldier. In A. McKenna (Ed.), *Buffalo soldier*. http://dx.doi.org/Buffalo soldier, nickname given to members of African American cavalry regiments of the U.S. Army who served in the western United States from 1867 to 1896, mainly fighting Indians on the frontier. The nickname was given by the Indians, but its significance is uncertain.

Carey, E. (2018). Psychosis. Retrieved from https://www.healthline. com/health/psychosis

Dr apj abdul kalam Evergreen quotes from his speeches. (2016). Retrieved from https://economictimes.indiatimes.com/people/ dr-apj-abdul-kalam-evergreen-quotes-from-his-speeches/slideshow/54867705.cms

Goalcast. (2017). 25 maya angelou quotes to inspire your life. Retrieved from https://www.goalcast.com/2017/04/03/ maya-angelou-quotes-to-inspire-your-life/

Harriett tubman historical society. (2020). Harriett tubman quotes. Retrieved from http://www.harriet-tubman.org/about-us/

Hayes, M. (2015). 8 kerry washington quotes that will totally inspire you. Retrieved from https://www.marieclaire.co.uk/entertainment/tv-and-film/8-kerry-washington-quotes-that-will-totally-inspire-you-84035

Hiatt, A. (2019, June 26). Who Were the Montford Point Marines? *JSTOR.* http://dx.doi.org/https://daily.jstor.org/who-were-the-montford-point-marines/

History.com Editors. (2009). Martin luther king jr. Retrieved from https://www.history.com/topics/black-history/martin-luther-king-jr

joe johnsonnkjlkvlm;n ;knv;kmvck;l (https://suozzi.house.gov/media/press-releases/suozzi-presents-us-flag-william-joe-johnson-tuskegee-airman-and-glen-cove)

King, L. A. (2013). Experience Psychology (2nd ed.). New York, NY: McGraw Hill.

Kniffel, L. (2011). Reading for life Oprah winfrey. Retrieved from https://americanlibrariesmagazine.org/2011/05/25/reading-for-life-oprah-winfrey/

Leadhem, R. (2018). 12 daymond john quotes to help you achieve greatness. Retrieved from https://www.entrepreneur.com/slideshow/308610

Marine Corps Riflemen's' Creed. (Retrieved from https://bootcamp4me.com/the-riflemans-creed/

Meah, A. (n.d.). 35 inspirational tyler perry quotes on success. Retrieved from https://www.awakenthegreatnesswithin.com/35-inspirational-tyler-perry-quotes-on-success/

Mother teresa quotes. (2020). Retrieved from https://www.catholic.org/clife/teresa/quotes.php

Only i can change my life no one carol burnett. (2020). Retrieved from https://inspire99.com/only-i-can-change-my-life-no-one-carol-burnett/

Post-traumatic stress disorder. (2019, August 7). Mayo Clinic. http://dx.doi.org/https://www.mayoclinic.org/diseases-conditions/post-traumatic-stress-disorder/symptoms-causes/syc-20355967

Psychosis. (). Healthline. http://dx.doi.org/https://www.healthline.com/health/psychosis#false-realities

Public Broadcasting Service. (n.d.). Napoleon the myth and the man. Retrieved from https://www.pbs.org/empires/napoleon/n_myth/self/page_1.html

quotes by malcolm X. (2020). Retrieved from https://www.malcolmx.com/quotes/

Ray, M. (2019, January 9). Harlem Hellfighters (Encyclopedia Britannica. http://dx.doi.org/https://www.britannica.com/topic/Harlem-Hellfighters)

Robertson, I. (2014, May 11). 10 Quotes From Diddy's Howard Commencement Speech. *Vibe*. http://dx.doi.org/https://www.vibe.com/2014/05/10-quotes-diddys-howard-commencement-speech

Rutstein, N. (, Spring 2009). Frontiers of healing racism. *ProQuest*, 9. http://dx.doi.org/https://search-proquest-com.ezproxy.liberty.edu/docview/214194589?pq-origsite=summon

Schizophrenia. (2019, February 14). Psychology Today. http://dx.doi.org/https://www.psychologytoday.com/us/conditions/schizophrenia

Sue, D. W., Sue, D., Neville, H. A., & Smith, L. (). Counseling the Culturally Diverse Theory and Practice (8th ed.). Hoboken, NJ: Wiley.

United States Marine Corps. (2020). Retrieved February 7, 2020, from https://www.britannica.com/topic/The-United-States-Marine-Corps

Williams, M. T. (2019, February 19). Uncovering the Trauma of Racism. American Psychological Association. http://dx.doi.org/https://www.apa.org/pubs/highlights/spotlight/issue-128

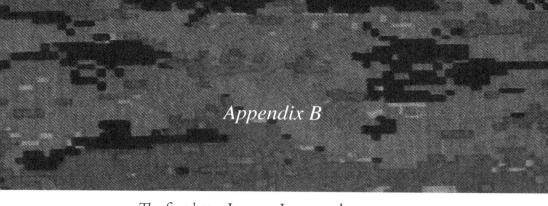

The first letter I sent to Jerome at boot camp

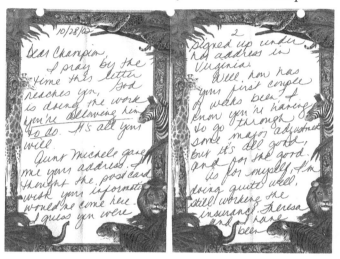

-5-

Jerome, you've been on your mothers prayers. Michele and I talked regarding the issue you have, I mean dealing with those young girls. Jerome you need to know in your spirit and your mind that God has something greater for your life. Don't let satan rob you of your blessings. Know that your mother

-6-

is praying on your behalf. Know that the enemy is a liar. Jerome, go back to those days you and I went to church together, remember what you saw God do in my life — in the parking lot when Katrina and the other woman ministered to me. Yet actually, God wanted you there to be a witness to

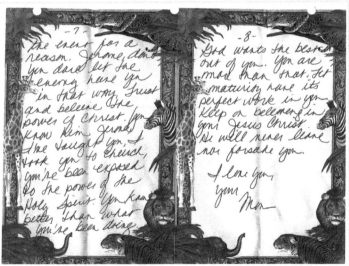

-7-

the enemy for a reason. Jerome, don't you dare let the enemy have you in that way. Trust and believe the power of Christ. You know Him Jerome, I the taught you, I took you to church, you've been exposed to the power of the Holy Spirit. You know better than what you've been doing.

-8-

God wants the best out of you. You are more than that. Let maturity have its perfect work in you. Keep on believing in your Jesus Christ. He will never leave nor forsake you.

I love you,
your
Mom

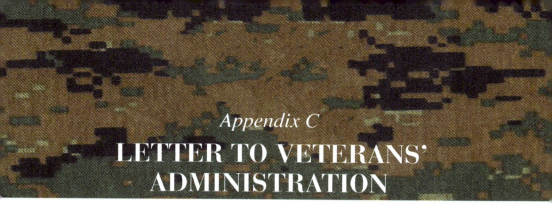

September 11, 2006

Mrs. Million Heir-Williams
(Mother of Jerome Brown)
627 Anywhere Ave.
Jacksonville, NC 28546

Department of Veterans Affairs
Regional Office
Federal Building
251 North Main Street
Winston-Salem, NC 27155-1000

Dear Sir or Madam:

I recall boot camp graduation and that day was one of excitement and a proud feeling seeing my son in uniform. A proud mother of a Marine of the United States of America. However, that all drastically changed once my son returned home from Iraq. Looking at him caused me severe pain because I was aware there was trauma he had experienced and was not adjusting properly here in the states.

One incident when he went "UA", he sent several text messages:

1st text May 4, 2005 @ 1:44 am, "Im alive mom forgive me I hate the marine corps I love you mother

2nd text May 12, 2005 @1:08 am, "I don't' mean to scare you but I will turn myself in im just worried about some of the voices."

3rd text May 12, 2005 @ 1:38 am, "If you wanna find him hes not to far from a small church jet lee is not the one expose the hawk and he will find the nest."

4th text May 12, 2005 @ 2:35 am, "Life is good but iraq was not some of the highways I drive remind me of Iraq highways like 17 and 24."

These text messages were his way of crying out for help. The text messages confirmed for me as his mother, there was something more seriously wrong with my son that I realized.

I began my mission through the Jacksonville Police Department. A detective was handling the case at the time. I feel to this date that my son was misdiagnosed by the United States Marine Corps. A time when he went UA my husband and I took him to the emergency Room on base, I wanted him admitted under psychiatric care. I knew he need medical treatment, and something was drastically wrong with my son, mentally! The doctor was going to release him and stated, "He has problems adjusting." I couldn't believe what I was hearing from this doctor. I stated, "Sir, if you release my son in his present condition and something happens to him, or somebody does something to him. I will go public with this type of treatment our military is receiving right here on our great land of the USA. After I mentioned this to the doctor, he finally admitted Jerome to 4Alpha ward and kept him for two weeks. I had several conversations with the staff and the psychiatrists he was assigned to at the time. He was admitted on May 18, 2005.

As a mother you know when something is different about your son. Now that my son has been properly diagnosed because of full mental breakdown six weeks after being released from the USMC, not by the military, however, I was forced to go outside of the military to get the proper diagnosis from a county facility. I repeatedly told, informed, communicated something is wrong with my son. All my labor of speech was in vain because he passed a final medical assessment upon being released from the military. Please for GOD's sake, please tell me in my right mind that any individual can be diagnosed six weeks after being released from the military, that a psychiatrist can diagnose an individual with "Bipolar, Manic Depressive Disorder and Severe Psychosis." This came about because my son had a complete mental breakdown and snapped in which I was forced to call the Jacksonville Police Department. Thank GOD one of the officers understood the dilemma we were up against because her spouse was dealing with certain issues (he had been deployed several times). My son finally calmed down, and they asked, "Would you like to drive your son to the Behavioral Center (do you feel safe?), or would you like us to take him?" "If we take him, by law we must handcuff." I immediately felt my son is not a criminal, "I informed the officer we will drive him, thank you." I was profoundly grateful for the officer's display of compassion. I was clear my son had this condition going on all last year when I did my best to inform the USMC. I knew no one believed me each time I went to the Camp Lejeune explaining that something was wrong with my son. All along desperately seeking the medical attention he needed.

He is currently being treated every two weeks by the Onslow Carteret Behavioral Healthcare Services (located at 215 Memorial Dr. Jacksonville, NC 28546 910.355.5118). He has been prescribed three different medications while they are trying to find the right dosage as well as the right medication. The following meds were prescribed: Geodon 40 mg, 2 Seroquel 200 mg, symbax (alazapine-12mg/fluoxetine-25mg. hci capsules).

My son is twenty-six years of age, he has tried to get a job. He was employed for two weeks and they let him go. I had the opportunity to speak with his boss and he informed me, "We all liked your son very much, but there were certain things going on we didn't understand. I coached him a few times, but it didn't work out." I explained the condition my son was dealing with at the time. Here is my son trying to work and be a productive citizen, however, with this mental condition it is impossible. What kind of life is this for anyone who is twenty-six years of age and unable to hold a job due to mental disorders??? Jerome never had any of these symptoms prior to joining the military and six weeks after being discharged he had a full mental breakdown. The government did not want any responsibility in his condition which is wrong and their lack of accountability to what's been caused by the USMC. This is uncivil behavior on the part of the military. If Jerome had been diagnosed six months from now, or six years later, then maybe you could question whether this was related to the military.

SIX WEEKS AFTER DISCHARGE AND MY SON HAS BEEN DIAGNOSED WITH SEVERAL MENTAL DISORDERS!

I NEED YOUR HELP – DESPERATLEY – ON BEHALF OF MY SON!!!

SINCERELY,
Million Heir-Williams

DELIVERANCE FROM SATAN AND HIS DEMONIC FORCES

Father, in the name of Jesus, I come boldly to Your throne of grace and present Jerome Bernard Milan Brown before you. I stand in the gap and intercede in behalf of Jerome knowing that the Holy Spirit within me takes hold together with me against the evils that would attempt to hold Jerome in bondage. I unwrap Jerome from the bonds of wickedness with my prayers and take the shield of faith and quench the fiery dart of the adversary that would come against Jerome Bernard Milan Brown.

Father, you say that whatever I bind on earth is in heaven, and whatever I loose on earth is loosed in heaven. You say for me to cast out demons in the name of Jesus.

So, I speak to you Satan, and the principalities, the powers, the rulers of darkness, and spiritual wickedness in high places and the demonic spirits of bipolar, manic depression, and psychosis assigned to Jerome Bernard Milan Brown. I take authority over you and bind you away from Jerome Bernard Milan Brown in the mighty name of Jesus. You loosen Jerome Bernard Milan Brown and let him go free in the name of Jesus. I demand that you stop your maneuvers now. Satan, you are a spoiled and defeated foe.

Ministering Spirits of God, you go forth in the name of Jesus and provide the necessary help and assistance for Jerome Bernard Milan Brown.

Father, I have laid hold of Jerome Bernard Milan Brown's salvation and his confession of Lordship of Jesus Christ. I speak of things that not as though they were, for I choose to look at the unseen—the eternal things of God. I say Satan shall not get an advantage over Jerome Bernard Milan Brown: for I am not ignorant of Satan's devices. I resist

Satan and he has run in terror from Jerome Bernard Milan Brown in the name of Jesus! I give Satan no place in Jerome Bernard Milan Brown. I plead the Blood of the Lamb over Jerome Bernard Milan Brown for Satan and his cohorts are overcome by the Blood and Your Word! I thank You, Father, that I tread on serpents and scorpions and over all the power of the enemy in Jerome Bernard Milan Brown's behalf. Jerome Bernard Milan Brown is delivered from this present evil world! He is delivered from the powers of darkness and translated into the Kingdom of Your dear Son, Christ our Lord and Savior!

Father, I ask You now to fill those vacant places within Jerome Bernard Milan Brown with Your redemption, Your Word, Your Holy Spirit, Your love, Your wisdom, Your righteousness, and Your revelation and knowledge in the name of Jesus.

I thank you, Father, that Jerome Bernard Milan Brown is redeemed by the blood of Jesus out of the hand of Satan. He is justified and made righteous by the blood of Jesus and belongs to You, spirit, soul, and body. I thank you that every enslaving yoke is broken, and he will not become slave of anything or be brought under its power, in the name of Jesus. Jerome Bernard Milan Brown has escaped the snare of the devil who has held him captive and henceforth does Your will, Father, which is to glorify You in his spirit, soul, and body.

Thank You, Father. Jesus was manifested that he might destroy the works of the devil. Satan's works are destroyed in Jerome Bernard Milan Brown's life, in the name of Jesus!

Hallelujah! Jerome Bernard Milan Brown walks in the Kingdom of God, which is righteousness, peace, and joy. Praise the Lord!

Once this prayer has been prayed, thank the Father that Satan and his cohorts are bound. Stand firm, fixed, immovable, and steadfast on my confessions of faith as I intercede on Jerome Bernard Milan Brown's behalf because I know there is a Greater one that lives on the inside of my son.

Author Unknown

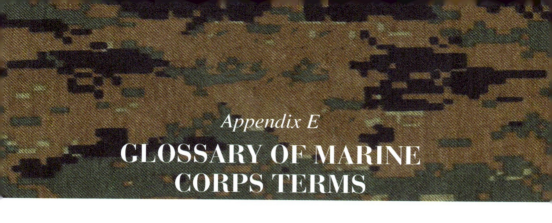

Appendix E
GLOSSARY OF MARINE CORPS TERMS

The United States Marine Corps—"A separate military service within the U.S. Department of the Navy, charged with the provision of marine troops for seizure and defense of advanced bases and with conducting operations on land and in the air incident to naval campaigns. It is also responsible for providing detachments for service aboard certain types of naval vessels, as well as security forces for naval shore installations and U.S. diplomatic missions in foreign countries. The corps specializes in amphibious landings, such as those undertaken against Japanese-held islands in the Pacific during World War II." (Encyclopedia Britannica, 2020, para. 1)

7 Tons—Gig vehicles

782 Gear—Items worn on your body, the components of the 782 are as follows: Kevlar helmet, Kevlar vest, Kevlar breastplates, cartridge belt and harness (holds canteens, ammunition pouches in the belt), and your pack (holds clothing, extra uniforms, boots, socks, underwear, meals ready to eat, and personal items.

Administrative Separation—Marines who are separated from military service for various reasons.

Armed Forces Vocational Aptitude Battery (ASVAB)—Entry exam for everyone entering the armed forces. Once the score has been determined, it will inform a soldier where he or she scored the highest on the exam and that person will be placed into a particular job category accordingly.

Artillery—Big guns

Unauthorized Leave of Absence or Absent Without Leave—Absent without leave for short or long term.

Barracks—Primary housing for the Marines.

Battalion—A unit of Marines of approximately six hundred personnel, including a wide array of military occupational jobs.

Battalion Commander—Field grade officer, usually a lieutenant or colonel

Battery Commander—Field grade officer, usually a lieutenant or colonel

Chain of Command—Hierarchy of command.

Chow—Food

Command—Order to be followed by one is superior

Command Post—Headquarters unit usually led by a commanding general or officer and staff advisory personnel to the commander. Also, it directs the actions of field units.

Commissioned Officer—A person entering the military with a bachelor's degree, or higher, commissioned by US Congress.

Count off—Ensure everyone is accounted for

Devil Dog—German name given to Marines who fought the battle of Belleau Woods in WWI.

Discharge of Active Duty (DD-214 form), which indicates proof of service
- Honorable Discharge
- General Discharge Under Honorable Conditions
- Other Than Honorable Discharge
- Bad Conduct Discharge
- Dishonorable Discharge

Deployment—Self-contained Marine units sent to various areas around the world to protect American interests

Duty Station— Marines deploy from duty stations.

Entry Control Point—Verify people entering the base

Enlisted member—Someone entering the military without a degree

Field Operations—Training

First Sergeant —Senior advisor to the company commander

Fleet—There are nine components, comprised of all Marine Corps units
1st Marine Division is located at Camp Pendleton, California
1. 1st Marine Aircraft Wing
2. 1st Marine Force Service Support Group
3. 2nd Marine Division is located at Camp Lejeune, North Carolina
   2nd Marine Aircraft Wing
   2nd Marine Force Service Support Group
   3rd Marine Division is located in Okinawa, Japan
   3rd Marine Aircraft Wing
   3rd Marine Force Service Support Group

Footlocker—Small wooden locker where Marines store their personal items and uniforms

Formation—Assembled group of Marines for accountability purposes

Government Issue (G.I.) – The individual Marine is government issue.

Grades—Different grades represent the pay chart.
- E: Enlisted Members
- W: Warrant Officers
- O: Officers with more than four years active duty as enlisted or Warrant Officers
- O: Commissioned Officers

Hazing—Strenuous, often humiliating, tasks as part of a program of rigorous physical training and initiation

Humvee—Large Jeep

Infantry—Commonly called grunts, frontline fighting force

Judge Advocate General—Marine Corps lawyers

Jarhead— This name was given to the Marines by the sailors during World War II because they made fun of their heads once they put on their dress blues (they said their head looked like a head sticking out of a mason jar.) Marines took it as a compliment.

Marine Combat Training – Training to become a Marine.

Mess Hall— Cafeteria

Military Occupational Specialty—A category of a military job, approximately forty-three different categories exist

    I.   Combat Arms
    II. Infantry
    III. Artillery
    IV. Special Weapons & Tactics
    V. Intelligence

Montford Point Marines—"The Commandant of the Marine Corps, among other officers, was vehemently opposed. As the march grew closer—and under pressure from his wife Eleanor—Roosevelt conceded. On June 25, 1941, just a week before the march was set to take place, the president signed Executive Order 8802, prohibiting racial discrimination in the defense industry or in government. At last, all branches of the U.S. Armed Forces were open to African Americans" (Hiatt, 2019, Chapter 1).

Non-Commissioned Officer—Small unit leaders middle management, usually a corporal or sergeant

Non-Judicial Punishment—Going before your commanding officer to receive punishment

Online—Standing at the position of attention

OOH-RAH—A battle cry for the Marines, WHICH came from World War I during the Battle of Belleau Woods

Open Contract—Given to a Marine recruit who has not requested or qualified for a Military Occupational Specialty.

Platoon— Small units made up of first, second, third, and fourth squads

Physical Fitness Test— Semi-annual fitness test to determine Marines combat readiness.

Physical Training—Is done every morning for about an hour and a half

Pit—Area used to discipline wayward recruit members or platoons

Quarterdeck—Naval ship term used in boot camp squad bay as the recruit assembly area

Racks—Beds

Rank Structure—Starts at private first class and goes all the way to general

Rifleman's Creed—This is my rifle. There are many like it, but this one is mine.
My rifle is my best friend. It is my life. I must master it as I must master my life.
Without me, my rifle is useless. Without my rifle, I am useless. I must fire my rifle true. I must shoot straighter than my enemy who is trying to kill me. I must shoot him before he shoots me. I will ...
My rifle and I know that what counts in war is not the rounds we fire, the noise of our burst, nor the smoke we make. We know that it is the hit that counts. We will hit ...
My rifle is human, even as I because it is my life. Thus, I will learn it as a brother. I will learn its weaknesses, its strength, its parts, its accessories, its sights, and its barrel. I will keep my rifle clean and ready, even as I am clean and ready. We will become part of each other. We will ...
Before God, I swear this creed. My rifle and I are the defenders of my country. We are the masters of our enemy. We are the saviors of my life. So be it, until victory is America's and there is no enemy, but peace!

School of Infantry— School where Marine Combat Training is taught

Semper Fidelis—Always faithful

Squad Bay—Housing unit used to house recruit platoons

Squad Leader—A small unit leader responsible for missions and recruit welfare

Staff Non-Commissioned Officer—An enlisted middle manager

Uniforms— Graduation: Dress Blue B (black coat and blue trousers for winter months) or Dress blue D (short-sleeved khaki shirt and blue trousers for summer months).

Theatre of Operation—An area where combat operations are conducted

Unit—Organization of Marines

Warrant Officer—Technical position for schools and trainings.

THE UNITED STATES MARINE CORPS

ENLISTED RANK STRUCTURE

<u>Learn to Develop and Grow</u>
Private
Private First Class
Lance Corporal

<u>Leadership Roles</u>
Corporal
Sergeant

<u>Senior Position</u>
Staff Sergeant
Gunnery Sergeant
Master Sergeant
First Sergeant
Master Gunnery Sergeant
Sergeant Major

T here are multiple organizations to assist veterans and family members. The governmental agencies are the first websites listed. Please take advantage of these groups. They are there to help bridge the gap and get you back to wholeness. It is your godly and constitutional right to live a healthy and normal life. You have earned all these benefits; they are not handouts. Not all of these websites are government agencies, so you may have to do supplemental research regarding the website. Furthermore, the websites were not chosen because I have relationships with them. God bless you and your family.

Headquarters US Marine Corps
Personnel Management Division MMSB-12
2008 Elliot Road
Quantico, VA 22134-5030
Official Business

Military Personnel Records (Request for administrative military records)
1 Archive Dr.
St Louis, MO 63138

Navy Medicine Records Activity (Request for military medical records)
BUMED Detachment-St. Louis
4300 Goodfellow Blvd. Bldg. 103
Saint Louis, MO 63120

VA.org

VA Court System
625 N. Washington St. #212
Alexandria, VA 22314
703.575.9400
https://www.lawforveterans.org/veterans-courts
https://justiceforvets.org/what-is-a-veterans-treatment-court/
U.S. Department of Health & Human Services–Substance Abuse &
Mental Health Services Administration
https://findtreatment.samhsa.gov/

Guide to VA Mental Health Services for Veterans & Families
https://www.mentalhealth.va.gov/docs/MHG_English.pdf

Most Vets Don't Know What Mental Health VA offers
https://taskandpurpose.com/mental-health-services-va

Benefits for Veterans
https://www.benefits.gov/benefit/4747

Supporting Providers who Serve Veterans
https://www.mirecc.va.gov/visn19/consult/?utm_source=Google-
Search&utm_medium=Option1&utm_campaign=SRM

Military One Source
https://www.blogs.va.gov/VAntage/51355/military-one-
source-now-available-veterans-families-full-year-separating-military-2/

Social Security Administration
(If a veteran is 100% disabled)

DAV.org

The Disabled American Veterans (DAV) is an organization created by the United States Congress for disabled military veterans of the United States Armed Forces.DAV
https://secure.dav.org/site/Donation2?df_id=10801&10801.donation=form1&gclid=CjwKCAiA66_xBRBhEiwAhrMuLeN-oTLU-ZCC1DT_UmCEiUmGqXHRZzyZpfy4EqOfVFYSv23XgzaFr1hoCqBEQAvD_BwE

National Alliance on Mental Health
https://nami.org/Get-Involved/Awareness-Events/Why-Care?gclid=CjwKCAiA66_xBRBhEiwAhrMuLektdVoanF-cUzj-BwTMzCMVlb3BNwBNkqqU9DUYa8IEb0xISA76D0ho-Cl3cQAvD_BwE

USO.org

LosAngelesTreatmentCenter.com 818.990.5901

Hudvash.com

Soldiers' Helpers–Care Packages for Our Deployed Heroes
https://justoursoldiershelpers.org/

Vetsandplayers.org

Anxiety.org

Help for Service Members & their Families
https://www.uso.org/programs?gclid=Cj0KCQiAyKrxBRDHARI-sAKCzn8wGxupiW_bh99eO4ntBsbr-JLFsQEMQX—7gxGXjpSN-ReBVv36qsukaAvytEALw_wcB
California Veterans Resource Book

www.calvet.ca.gov
800.952.5626

Cultural Competency for Serving the Military & Veterans
https://www.samhsa.gov/section-223/cultural-competency/
military-veterans

Operation Homefront
https://www.operationhomefront.org/
https://www.veteransadvantage.com/giving-back/
trusted-military-organizations-and-nonprofits

The Homefront Club (Book-Marine)–www.cinchouse.com
Strategic Behavioral Center (North Carolina) 855.537.2262
www.sbcwilmington.com
www.ncveteransworkinggroup.org (North Carolina)

Take a mental health quiz
ttps://www.psycom.net/quizzes
www.healthdiaries.com/bipolar-disorder.htm

President Trump Signs Executive Order for Veterans
https://www.veteransadvantage.com/blog/discounts-benefits/presi-
dent-donald-j-trump-signs-executive-order-improve-mental-health
Additional Resources for Service Members, Veterans & Military Families
https://ag.ny.gov/consumer-frauds/
additional-resources-service-members-and-veterans

Lifeline for Vets
https://nvf.org/lifeline-for-vets/

Life Springs Health System
http://www.lifespringhealthsystems.org/

www.mhsource.com/bipolar
www.nami.org/template.cfm

The Military Wallet
https://themilitarywallet.com/

Military
www.moveon.org

Iraq and Afghanistan of America
https://iava.org/
www.nimh.org

International Mental Health
https://www.psycom.net/get-help-mental-health

Mental Health First Aid
https://www.mentalhealthfirstaid.org/wp-content/uploads/2019/11/
Mental-Health-First-Aid-Adults-One-Pager_2019.pdf

Child & Family Guidance Center
Child Guidance.org

Videos

Elliot McKenzie–Gunshots (Feat. The Marine Rapper)
https://www.youtube.com/watch?v=Eh2pY55s89s
https://www.youtube.com/samhsa/
https://www.ptsd.va.gov/appvid/video/index.asp
https://www.ptsd.va.gov/appvid/video/index.asp

Articles

https://atwar.blogs.nytimes.com/2012/02/24/new-study-gives-scope-
and-cost-of-combat-related-conditions-among-veterans/

11 Facts About Military Families

https://docs.google.com/document/d/16ZKAkZd3tx-9li1U7KDT7DafrdDMzqPEHuTyplE9HwXY/edit?folder=1A3YTAPb9lfyLv8VWDteHHXPORAptsRT6#

Services for the Military

Massage therapist who has worked with veterans

El Deana Pearson Massages

Peace-Love.massagetherapy.com

Eat.love.massage@gmail.com

661.729.2100

43713 20th St.

Lancaster, CA 93534

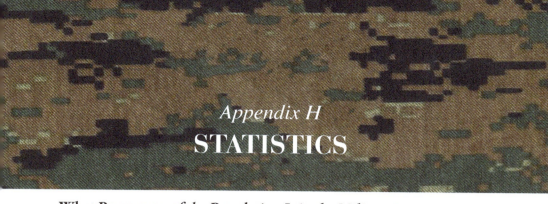

Appendix H
STATISTICS

What Percentage of the Population Is in the Military?
At the time, the active component of the **military** comprised 2.2 million men and women. Now, this group comprises just under 1.29 million, or less than 0.5 **percent** of the U.S. **population**. Apr. 24, 2018
Demographics of the U.S. Military | Council on Foreign Relations
https://www.cfr.org > article > demographics-us-military

How Many Soldiers Are in the US Military in 2019?
As of **2019**, the **U.S.** spends **US**$693 billion to fund its armed forces mandatory and discretionary accounts. As of 2018, the **U.S.** constitutes roughly 36 percent of the world's **military** expenditures.
The United States Armed Forces–Wikipedia
https://en.m.wikipedia.org > wiki > United States Armed Forces

How Many People Will retire from the Military?
By 2029, the number of **military** retirees in the United States is expected to reach 2.21 million; an increase from an estimated 2.17 million retirees in 2019. Nov 7, 2019
• U.S.–forecast number of military retirees 2029 | Statista
https://www.statista.com > statistics > forecast-number-of-military-retirees-in-...

How Many Military Kids Join the Military?
There are approximately 1.9 million **military children**, ranging in ages from newborn to 18 years old, 1.3 million **military children** are school-aged. 765,000 of our **military children** have Active duty parents, and approximately 225,000 have a parent who is currently deployed. Apr 5, 2012

The month of the Military Child: Saluting Our Military Children ...
https://www.dodlive.mil › 2012/04/05 ›
month-of-the-military-child-saluting...

List Veteran Suicide Rates by State
https://onceasoldier.org/veteran-suicide-rates-by-state/?gclid=Cj0KC-
QiAgKzwBRCjARIsABBbFujX49lNCctwRovPsmWiYiCEnz1cjqw-
pHkgRSVCPWy0nwkTErlyZtfcaApeWEALw_wcB
Suicide Surpasses War as Leading Cause of Death
https://readersupportednews.org/news-section2/318-66/27389-sui-
cide-surpasses-war-as-leading-cause-of-us-military-deaths

What is the Divorce Rate for the Military?
According to other studies, deployed **military** members in the U.S. Navy,
Marines, **Army** and Air Force have higher than average **divorce rates.**
The Air Force had the highest **rate**, at 14.6 percent, with the Navy at
over 12.5 percent. Mar 1, 2018
Why Is the Divorce Rate for Military So High? | LawInfo Blog
https://blog.lawinfo.com › 2018/03/01 ›
why-is-the-divorce-rate-for-military...

What Percentage of Military Marriages End in Divorce?
Although the overall **divorce** rate hasn't changed dramatically, the rate
of **marriage** in the **military** has seen a steady decline, according to
Defense Department data compiled by **Military**.com. In fiscal 2017,
about 51.7 **percent** of all active-duty troops were **married**, compared
to 56.6 **percent** in 2011. Mar 21, 2018
Troop Divorce Rate Unchanged; Marriage Rate ...–Military.com
https://www.military.com › daily-news › 2018/03/21 ›
troop-divorce-rate-un...

Domestic Violence in the Military

https://www.womenslaw.org/laws/federal/domestic-violence-military/all

Domestic Violence in the Military

https://vawnet.org/sites/default/files/assets/files/2016-09/DVMilitary.pdf

Alcohol Abuse in the Military

https://www.military.com/daily-news/2019/04/11/us-military-americas-heaviest-drinking-profession-survey-finds.html

Million **Heir-Williams** was born in Glen Cove, New York. At the age of twenty, she moved to Los Angeles, California, where she worked in management for Kaiser Permanente for twenty years. In 2004, she moved to Onslow County, North Carolina to become a co-owner of a family-owned and operated business. To complete the circle, Million moved back to California in 2018 with her husband, Dr. Stephen J. Williams. They reside in Lancaster with their two fur babies. They share a blended family of eight children and fifteen grandchildren.

In 2012, Million and Stephen founded The Remnant Fellowship Ministries where they are both pastors. The mandate for the ministry is "To eradicate biblical illiteracy."

As a former business owner of Kingdom Family Creations, Million joined the Jacksonville-Onslow Chamber of Commerce. The chamber recognized her exceptional leadership skills and created a Vice President role for her for meeting the goals and objectives of the organization.

Million is the founder and President of Seven Times Anointed Ministries International (STAMI); a nonprofit organization, which was a ministry, designed to bring hope, healing, freedom and restoration to women, their families and communities.

Million was appointed as a member of the Onslow County Board of Commissioners for two years, from January 2014 to December 2016. Former North Carolina Governor, Pat McCrory, appointed Million to serve on the Board of Directors for the North Carolina Council for Women in October 2014.

Million began Effectual Life Coaching (ELC) operations in Lancaster, California in 2018. She has a proven record of establishing rich, equitable relationships, which prove to be successful with everyone involved. She received her certification as a Life Growth Coach in 2016. Additionally, she has a Lean Six Sigma Yellow Belt, and is an Image-Esteem Consultant. Presently she is working with several non-profit organizations and entrepreneurs to enhance their business initiatives. ELC is a member of the following organizations: Lancaster Chamber of Commerce, Soroptimist Antelope Valley, AV Holistic Chamber of Commerce, Hispanic Chamber of Commerce and Team Referral Network, Society for Collegiate Leadership & Achievement, Worldwide Association of Female Professionals, American Psychological Association, American Association of Christian Counselors, Fellow of the North Carolina Institute of Political Leadership, and the Citizens Commission on Human Rights International.

Million is currently attending Liberty University online. She is pursuing her Bachelor of Science degree in psychology with an emphasis on life coaching. In addition, she studied business management through Phoenix University.

Million is available for speaking engagements and book tours. Below her contact information is available if you are interested in any of her services.

Order your book at www.MilitaryMomonaMission.us.
sales@militarymomonamission.us
323.435.6789

For Life Coaching Services:
www.EffectualLifeCoaching.com
info@effectualifecoaching.com
323.435.6789

STAY CONNECTED TO OUR MILITARY!

CPSIA information can be obtained
at www.ICGtesting.com
Printed in the USA
JSHW041002220720
6826JS00004B/16